C000154694

"This book sets out a firm found[
Christian engagement in public lii

Julian Rivers, *Ph.D.,*
Professor of Jurisprudence
University of Bristol

"In an arena where Christian activism can lack robust theological justification, it is great to see this clear and considered biblical outline for evangelical public theological engagement. *Good News for the Public Square* is a solid introduction to these important issues."

Dan Strange, *Ph.D.,*
Academic Vice Principal & Tutor
in Culture, Religion and Public Theology,
Oak Hill College

"It is vitally important that Christians are involved in the public square but that involvement needs to be biblically faithful, theologically rigorous, Christ-centred, gospel-hearted and a practical expression of our call to love God and neighbour. This resource provides a wonderful guide to those seeking to find common Christian ground in such characteristics of engagement with law and government. It needs to be widely read and integrated into our thinking and action as Christians."

Andrew Goddard, *Ph.D.,*
Associate Director,
Kirby Laing Institute for Christian Ethics (KLICE)
based within Tyndale House, Cambridge

"An excellent resource. It is extremely thoughtful and challenging. A real, positive contribution to debate and practice."

Nola Leach,
Chief Executive,
CARE

"This volume manages to stand back and think both broadly and deeply – and it encourages readers to do likewise. Rather than simply baptising received categories for thinking about public life, it develops four authentic theological ideas – authority, truth, goodness, and hope – using them to build up an argument for the way in which Christians can and should engage in public life. The result is considered, informative, and encouraging."

Nick Spencer,
Research Director,
Theos – the public theology think tank

"This book does not seek to provide all the answers for Christians concerned about issues of public policy and law – indeed it recognises that Christians will differ on the conclusions to be reached. What it sets out to do is to provide a framework of common ground from which it should be possible to approach such issues in order to further some serious thinking, analysis and discussion. Realistic conclusions may then emerge with some consensus, which will demonstrate the love of God and of his people for the community, by identifying the common good which is achievable in a secular culture. This is a helpful and encouraging book which I commend to all those who practics in, and seek to work out God's purposes in, the law in our pluralistic society."

The Hon. Mr. Justice Cooke,
High Court of Justice of England and Wales,
Judge in Charge of the Commercial Court (2012-13)

"The gospel, which is the power of God to salvation, saves real people. In this sense, the gospel is private. But, is the gospel only private? Should the faith be therefore privatised? Are there public implications for this powerful faith? Make no mistake: Jesus saves us *from* something *for* something. A purely privatised gospel fails to be the powerful gospel depicted scripturally. Read *Good News for the Public Square* and begin to explore *how* and *why*."

Jeffery J. Ventrella, *J.D., Ph.D.,*
Senior Counsel, Senior Vice-President,
Alliance Defending Freedom

The Lawyers' Christian Fellowship

GOOD NEWS FOR THE PUBLIC SQUARE

A Biblical Framework for Christian Engagement

CONTRIBUTORS

MIKE OVEY
Principal, Oak Hill College, London

WAYNE GRUDEM
*Research Professor of Theology and Biblical Studies,
Phoenix Seminary, Arizona, USA*

JONATHAN CHAPLIN
Director, Kirby Laing Institute for Christian Ethics, Cambridge

DAVID McILROY
Associate Research Fellow, Spurgeon's College, London

TIMOTHY LAURENCE
European Director, The Veritas Forum

*Edited by Timothy Laurence
on behalf of The Lawyers' Christian Fellowship*

GOOD NEWS FOR THE PUBLIC SQUARE
© Timothy Laurence, 2014.

Timothy Laurence has asserted his right under the Copyright,
Designs and Patents Act, 1988 to be identified as the author of this work.

First published in Great Britain in 2014
by The Lawyers' Christian Fellowship.
Email: admin@lawcf.org
www.lawcf.org

ISBN (paperback): 978-0-9506454-3-8
ISBN (kindle): 978-0-9506454-4-5
ISBN (ePub): 978-0-9506454-5-2

Typesetting and cover design by owen@daily.org.uk

Printed and bound by
Ashford Colour Press Ltd, Gosport, Hants PO13 0FW

Cover illustration: adapted from *Meyers Kleines Konversationslexikon.*
Fünfte, umgearbeitete und vermehrte Auflage. Bd. 1. Bibliographisches Institut,
Leipzig und Wien 1892. [Public domain], via Wikimedia Commons.

Contents

Preface

This study grew out of discussion and lecture seminars within the Lawyers' Christian Fellowship (LCF), currently comprising over 2,500 Christian lawyers, judges, law lecturers and law students in the United Kingdom.

The LCF hosted a lecture series in London during the election year of 2010. The issue at hand was the relationship between the gospel and the public square – how familiar biblical concepts fit together in a coherent framework.

Good News for the Public Square represents a collaborative project. The lecture series and titles were suggested by Tim Laurence in his role at that time as chairman of the LCF's London committee. He then discussed the outline with the four lecturers themselves who provided their content and delivered the lecture material, plotting the co-ordinates of a consistent framework.

Public Authority: 'God's servant for your *good*'.
Rev Dr Mike Ovey, Principal of Oak Hill College, former Parliamentary draftsman, co-author of Pierced for Our Transgressions;[1]

Public Truth: How can we *know* what is 'good'?
Dr David McIlroy, practising barrister, Head of Banking and Finance at 3 Paper Buildings; Visiting Senior Lecturer in Banking Law at SOAS (University of London); Associate Research Fellow, Theology of Law and Justice, at Spurgeon's College, London; author of A Biblical View of Law and Justice,[2] *and* A Trinitarian Theology of Law;[3]

Public Good: So what *is* 'good' for society?
Dr Jonathan Chaplin, political philosopher, Director of the Kirby Laing Institute for Christian Ethics (based within Tyndale House, Cambridge), co-editor of God and Government, *author of* Herman Dooyeweerd – Christian Philosopher of State and Civil Society;[4]

Public Hope: How can this 'good' be *achieved*?
Dr Wayne Grudem, Research Professor of Theology and Biblical Studies, Phoenix Seminary, Arizona, author of numerous books including Systematic Theology[5] *and* Politics According to the Bible.[6]

Each lecture was followed by feedback, questions and helpful discussion from the LCF membership. To conclude the series Tim then summarised the material, presenting it as a single lecture highlighting the framework provided by the series, with a prologue, introduction and conclusion for the LCF. In response, the LCF suggested that his paper should become the basis of this publication for a similar audience. Accordingly, Tim expanded that outline by re-incorporating original lecture material to produce a single piece as the draft for this book.

Collaboration continued as each of the four lecturers then generously commented on and approved the accounts of their own lectures presented here. Direct quotations from the live lectures are quoted verbatim where appropriate and indicated as such. However, for the sake of a more accessible publication as a single piece, the original lecture material has been variously summarised, expanded or revised, with additional material added where necessary. As such, the book is the result of collaborative work between Tim and the four lecturers as respective co-contributors, while the responsibility for the authorship of the final text is Tim's alone, as editor on behalf of the LCF.

The LCF is very grateful to each of the contributors for their support of the Fellowship, for making their material available to us for this purpose, and for their generous subsequent assistance in the preparation of the text.

The LCF is also very grateful to its members, staff and trustees for whom this project exists, and without whose experience and financial support the written project could not have taken shape.

Our hope is that this project will help God's people to serve him better by its record of our progress so far, and that its shortcomings will inspire them to improve on it as we all continue to grow in our understanding together year by year.

Tim Laurence studied English Literature at Oxford before working as a banking regulation lawyer at a global law firm in London. Based at Tyndale House in Cambridge, he is currently completing a ThM in Historical Theology from Westminster Theological Seminary (Philadelphia), while commencing with The Veritas Forum as European Director.

Overview

Purpose

Good News for the Public Square has been written to encourage us as Christians to love God and our neighbours through a biblically-shaped contribution to public life. It seeks to help Christians co-operate more effectively by providing a clear biblical framework to show how good government relates to the good news of Jesus Christ.

What is the relationship between Jesus Christ and the law of the land? To some this topic can seem too complex for useful discussion. To others it seems too self-evident. So we may either take no action at all in the public square (and keep the peace) or rush into action and divide ourselves without knowing why.

So this book clarifies orthodox biblical foundations – establishing the common framework around which we can work together and build toward more specific applications. It offers a common language for further conversation, education and activity. In matters of political thought there will always be diversity of opinion, but Bible-believing Christians share more than they realise. By using the same language and seeing the links between basic concepts we can identify and resolve apparent differences, and work together constructively. By following key stages of reasoning in an argument we can isolate key junctions of thought and learn from one another with respect in a way which will result in more effective action.

Good News for the Public Square has been written especially for Christians who are familiar with the Bible and who influence others – whether in the church or the public square. It is a theological framework not a practical agenda. However, each chapter implicitly suggests an agenda for further detailed theological or policy work in specific topic areas – such as the limits of state authority, the good of freedom or family, or the art of realistic and winsome lobbying. It is hoped that as readers grasp the gospel's framework for public life they can then lead further work toward practical applications in their own particular fields, contexts and congregations.

Conclusion

Because God has first loved us, we too should serve others by engaging in the public square – with *practical love, shaped by the gospel, wisely deployed*. This is good for everyone and it promotes the spread of the gospel.

Practical love...

As Christians we should love our neighbours by getting involved in public life in such a way as to benefit society and encourage human flourishing. This is love with *content* – not just 'the thought that counts' or our best guess as to what is needed.

This means we should contribute to public life in a way that works *with* the grain of God's loving design for human life. The Bible gives Christians unique insight into God's created pattern for thriving humanity within his creation. Since we have this knowledge we should help society choose to move toward this pattern. So of course this doesn't imply that we should 'enforce' a uniquely religious morality on irreligious people – as if we could! Nor does it imply we should generally rely on biblical language in public life in order to reach these goals, or necessarily do it in the name of the church, or simply promote the 'Christian interest' as a minority interest group. On the contrary, since God is Creator it means we can promote a *universal* pattern for the way that human life works best, and do so using the best evidence from God's world around us to support it. Love suggests that we should contribute actively, accessibly and persuasively to discussions within the public square, including on matters of law and policy.

Our policy goal as Christians is to bring about a welcoming acceptance of what is most beneficial for society. Human sin means none of us always wants to follow what is in our best interests. But the more the gospel spreads in society, the more people do welcome what actually works best. This means we need to recognise that only the spread of the gospel can change hearts and minds for the long-term. However, since our mandate is to love God and neighbour then we will not wait for a future generation before getting involved to help people practically today – and our love is the best endorsement for the gospel message.

Christians in the public square should assess what is practically achievable in the light of the situation, bearing in mind the health of that culture's common conscience and the historical effects of the gospel on its thinking. This requires wisdom and sensitivity. We should seek justice everywhere, while remembering it is counterproductive to try to make laws that society can't bear. Only the good news of Christ gives the ultimate foundation for good government and good character. Good government in turn protects the freedom to spread the gospel. The two are interconnected as part of God's greater story, and in God's design, each should complement the other.

...shaped by the gospel...

The love of God gives life and offers his gospel without discrimination. God does not restrict rain to the fields of Christians alone but he graciously sustains all human life. God has graciously instituted civil government to help human life through temporal justice and the restraint of evil. Similarly, Christian contribution to public life should be grace-shaped – for everyone's benefit – not just for other believers. The gospel also includes a call to repentance and to recognise Christ as Lord. Likewise, practical love demands that we oppose injustice boldly and highlight the harmful consequences of policies which contradict what is good. We are called to be gracious not moralistic, bringing substance over spin, backbone under pressure, courage in the face of evil, and offering hope to those in the grip of despair.

As Christians we need to rely on the gospel to help us love like this. Jesus showed his love for us, who were his enemies, so that by his death on the cross our sins could be forgiven, and we could inherit the new creation. This gospel changes our hearts as believers to give us deeper love for our society, and it also makes sense of God's design for his creation. It is only when we are reconciled to God and born again that we can fully recognise and welcome the way God has ordered his world. Until this point we all have some natural knowledge of what's good for our lives and what good government should aim for – but because of human sinfulness we are limited in our thinking and we don't always recognise or want the things which will be best for us. When we turn to Christ we can better recognise, and greet, God's life-giving ways for humanity. We can then seek to imitate his public love, even for his enemies, and do so in the power of the Holy Spirit.

...wisely deployed.

Proverbs teaches that "the fear of the LORD is the beginning of wisdom". Our highest priority is to honour God faithfully in our public engagement, knowing that this will also benefit society most. This means we should follow God's lead in the way he has already delegated and arranged for his work to be done. How is this? Or, we could introduce the question another way. Christianity benefits the public square by its heart-and-mind-transforming gospel message and by the substantive involvement of Christians in public activity. How has God arranged for these two to work together?

As an institution the church has been given the divine commission to preach the comprehensive gospel message and so make and grow disciples in the world over which Christ is Lord. Its activity facing the world is to be directed to that end: it bears God's word, which is the sword of the Spirit reaching hearts. Conversely, as an institution, civil government has been given the commission to use temporal authority in society to promote good and restrain evil – to do justice by law. Its discussions and judgments are to be embodied in that action: it bears the outward sword of justice.

Christian individuals, charities and organisations should take account of their calling and situation to determine whether their respective contribution at any given point is to be more directed toward assisting the proclamation of the gospel or assisting the action of civil government – and to ensure that these two, while complementary, do not become confused.

This may require churches to establish separate charitable entities where a primary focus on public action is required, thus enabling the church itself, and its overseers, to prioritise the preaching of the gospel. Their faithful Bible teaching on Sundays will nonetheless envision and equip their own members to serve their society in love during the rest of the week, in their own vocations and charitable endeavours. Likewise there will be circumstances where it is most helpful for Christian politicians, civil servants or charities to keep their vocational focus on biblical action rather than on biblical language – where it is better to see a biblical policy adopted than try to draw attention to the way this policy relates to the Bible. Such vocations, while rightly pursued out of service to the Lord of all, do not in themselves represent the church and its gospel, and should not be thought to do so.

Such case-by-case wisdom prevents the gospel being undermined through its becoming wrongly identified with law. It also prevents biblical public service being hindered by an insistence that it should only be rendered in the name of Christianity or not at all. This wisdom allows us to love our neighbours maximally, both in word and action, to the greater glory of the Sovereign Lord.

The framework behind the conclusion

The gospel itself is the Christian's framework for good government.

God's rule in creation

God's rule is the context for ours. Amongst other things, the gospel is the story of God's rule over creation being re-established through humanity. Adam and his family were to rule as the Sovereign God's representatives on earth, but this was frustrated because of Adam's rebellion. But the Bible tells us about Christ, another man whom God has appointed King to succeed where Adam failed.

In simple terms, both Adam and Christ give us a basic pattern for rule. In Eden, Adam cared for the garden and he also named the animals God brought to him. This involved seeing the world as it was and then using God's authority to bring and sustain good order. Similarly God, in Christ, took account of a world in need, and came with authority to bring salvation through justice, tackling evil and restoring good. He did this partly at this first coming, does it partly now through his gospel message and the accompanying work of the Spirit, and he will do it finally when he returns.

The public 'square': four elements of government

Notice that these paradigms of rule in God's world share four basic elements, reflecting four aspects of created space-time reality. They each involve: (i) a role with authority, (ii) a true assessment of the present situation, (iii) an understanding of what a good state of affairs should look like, and (iv) a view of how the situation is to be moved from its present state to that which is hoped for. Rule requires authority, truth, goodness and hope.

Since God has shaped reality in a consistent way, we find these four basic questions of government continually recur in political life today:

1. Authority: what is the role of the authorities?
2. Truth: how shall we know what is true about society?
3. Goodness: what is our substantive vision of flourishing life for human society?
4. Hope: what what is the way to get from here to there?

Whether they recognise it or not, public authorities operate with working assumptions as answers to these questions. They use certain authority to bring the hope of justice through judgment which to some extent defends and encourages what they believe is good. This is how God sovereignly uses public authorities to bless his creation, to reflect something of his rule, and to sustain orderly life on earth while the gospel spreads and prepares people for the final judgment.

Distortion through the fall

In a messy world we don't find the public square is shaped as it should be. Although these four questions are integral to rule in God's creation, the fall has affected the human heart and mind. This means that humanity has only a limited and confused understanding of these four concepts, especially in their origins and their ultimate ends. This confusion, combined with on-going sinfulness, has often resulted in an exaggerated autocratic role for human political authority – the ruler himself becomes the purported origin and goal of each of these things. In this situation the public square does not hang rightly within the story of God's own rule, and might only offer limited stability or actively harm people. It may also restrict the spreading of the gospel of Christ's government.

One of our privileges as Christians is to be part of the shaping of our own public square so that it does its God-given job more helpfully, rightly sitting within the greater story of God's own rule, and benefitting more people. How should we do this?

Light of the gospel

The gospel of Christ gives unique insight amid this confusion. The Gospels show that Jesus came as the Messiah. He is the awaited King of Israel who would fulfil what Israel's kingdom anticipated – the hope of 'promised land' restoration for all creation. The ultimate scope of Christ's work includes not only a restoration of humanity's relationship to God the Father, but also, through that reconciliation, a restoration of God's rule through humanity over the whole world.

John's Gospel in particular highlights the continuity between Christ's roles as Creator and as Redeemer. It does so through a focus on the identity of Christ as the Son of God, which is not only a reference to Christ's deity, but also to the status of the Messiah. His miraculous signs show that the life that he brings is not only the life of creation being restored, but it is at the same time the eternal life of knowing God as Father. The emphasis is on comprehensive abundance, and the story of God's kingdom is the story of reality.

Christ is the light of the world in every sense – including with respect to the sides of the public square. Notice how these themes are echoed in his words: "I AM the way, the truth and the life." (John 14:6). Incarnate in Christ is authority (echoing the LORD's name, "I AM"), truth, goodness ("life") and hope ("the way"). These four themes come from the Son of God in creation and move toward the same royal Son in redemption. In between, they are explored and developed throughout the whole Bible.

Hence we should recognise that the gospel has significant implications for political theory. Since each of these four concepts belongs to Christ and only makes sense in relation to him, the same is true of political theory as a whole. Christ's work in fulfilment of Israel's kingdom opens our eyes to what authority, truth, goodness and hope really mean in the story of the universe. It shows them in their real colours. We can then use this insight in navigating the murkier world of the human kingdoms.

Government and the gospel

If the concepts of authority, truth, goodness and hope are continuous between creation and its redemption, what is the distinction between earthly kingdoms and God's kingdom?

One significant aspect to the answer is that God has given a *limited mandate* to earthly public authorities: their mandate is not to bring about the new creation from changed hearts to a transformed universe – this is the mandate of King Jesus alone. Instead, the concern of earthly authorities is to do justice in public life within this creation. This brings a number of implications for Christians working in the public square, of which here are two:

First, we can navigate day-to-day complexities by understanding our own individual roles in relation to the limited role of government. We relate to earthly government primarily through its *man-*

date, while we relate to God's coming kingdom primarily through its *message*. Core to a mandate is the requirement that effective action should take place; it is secondary whether or not its full significance is understood. Conversely, core to a message is the communication of its rational content, and it is secondary whether certain action thereby results. When we speak of the way that authority, truth, goodness and hope only make sense because of Jesus, we are then beginning to share the gospel message, and so true political theorising rightly takes us toward Christ. But an exhaustive meta-political theory is not necessarily essential to undertake a limited and specific mandate in substantive terms at a given moment. So, on the other hand, when we merely apply these same four realities in practice to the world around us, we nonetheless engage in truly biblical political activity. This is the case regardless of whether we use specifically religious language and whether or not we explain our ultimate reasons for our actions or their prospects for long-term sustainability within our culture.

Second, we have flexibility in our use of language in the public square. If the mandate of government concerns effective action in this age then political authority is limited to the concerns of this creation. In turn this means that biblical wisdom about the world around us can be shared in the accessible language of God's creation which everybody shares. Biblical political contribution does not require special religious jargon. For example, some aspects of our four themes could be applied through taking positions such as the following: "Political authority should be limited and should not restrict basic human freedoms"; "Policy should be based on transparent evidence about the world as it really is"; "We can't enjoy a coherent rights-based framework without a shared understanding of what is good"; "Effective action takes account of the character of the people in question". These are conclusions yielded by the gospel of God's kingdom, but they are expressed in the universal language of creation. In this way we can bring an authentically biblical contribution to the public authority which God's common grace has provided for everyone's benefit, regardless of their faith.

As far as political action is concerned, our aim is to use a biblical understanding of authority, truth, goodness and hope to help the instituted human authorities do their job – to help the four sides of our own public square to straighten out increasingly in parallel with those of the story of God's kingdom, within which it all hangs. We must do so alongside the institutional church's essential mandate to preach the gospel for eternal life, knowing also that life in this age is only truly enjoyed, re-ordered and sustained when people are born again and believe that Jesus is the King of Israel, the Son of God.

The outline of the argument

The book is structured to 'show the working' behind the framework. Our hope is that this will draw attention to its critical junctions of thought, allowing discussion and encouraging further development and application.

After an illustrative prologue, the introduction starts with the basics: God's love for his whole creation. He freely gives everyone sun, rain and seasons for the sake of continued life on earth. The same love has also instituted public authorities for our good. As Christians we should recognise God's loving provision by helping public authorities to fulfil their God-given role, and where necessary calling them back to it. By God's sovereign wisdom this will also contribute to the spread of the gospel. But what is the role of the public authorities?

Chapter 1 – Public Authority: 'God's servant for your good'

We only recognise the proper purpose and limit of political authority by its accountability to the LORD's greater authority and kingdom, inherited by Christ, the incarnate I AM. Without this context, human political authority always overreaches itself, toward an oppressive godlike status. Its proper limitations are established in the gospel of a greater King. So what is the God-given role of the civil authorities? Starting with Romans 13 we see that it is to love society by using limited and accountable authority to encourage what is good for society and to restrain what harms it – the true meaning of the rule of law. But how shall we *know* what is good for society?

Chapter 2 – *Public Truth: how can we know what is 'good'?*

The pursuit of human knowledge is possible because the universe has been created coherently through Christ, the *logos*. This means that there is a pre-existing 'format' in reality which is shared by those who are observing and those who are observed. We can be confident that knowledge and truth, far from being an illusion, can be the basis of political judgment. This 'common sense knowledge' and scientific study relies on 'general revelation' from Christ in creation. But this knowledge is twisted and limited by our human sin and ignorance, so we need the Bible to clarify and extend our understanding of the world as it is. The story of Christ's incarnation not only reveals God through his person, but it also unlocks the whole Bible so that we can understand how God's law specifies what is really good for society. What then is the biblical *content* of this 'good' for society?

Chapter 3 – *Public Good: so what is 'good' for society?*

Everyone experiences goodness simply by virtue of being alive in God's creation which was made through Christ and was "very good" – "in him was life". We enjoy God's goodness most when we live in accordance with his design for us. God has patterned this in his law for the promised land, where – carefully interpreted in the light of Christ – we find the Bible's most detailed paradigm of a flourishing society. Good law today accords with this design, pointing society to what is best for us: protecting what God has made good, and defending that good from harm. The Ten Commandments can be read as a ten-point summary of key protections and principles for a flourishing society. But we can only truly want, enjoy and pursue God's goodness when we know the life of God in our hearts through Christ's gospel. How is society to attain this vision of goodness, and put wrongs, right?

Chapter 4 – *Public Hope: how can this 'good' be achieved?*

The gospel is the story of Christ who brings ultimate deliverance to humanity. This gospel also brings analogous political benefits in this world organically, wherever it spreads.

The gospel's implication for those in authority is that they should do justice. This begins with the humility of recognising that they themselves are not the Messiah. Such a fear of God leads to a practical wisdom and integrity for good and impartial rule, when they recognise God's laws are the ground of true justice both for themselves and for society. The wider gospel story also gives practical realism when we recognise the limitations of political power, and the importance of the character of society as a whole in order to accept good law and to co-operate with justice. Justice is right action to punish those who have brought harm and restore situations towards what is good.

The story of Christ's own kingdom highlights the condition of the human heart as a key factor in the way he rules. Similarly, good government takes account of the hearts of the people it serves. It does not pursue a naive humanistic Utopia or accelerate its work more quickly than the people can bear. It does not force laws upon a people which they cannot accept. Such moves are counterproductive, ignoring the presence and pattern of God's greater kingdom. As such, the possibilities of good government progress and recede in connection with the spread or withdrawal of the gospel in society. The gospel's implication for Christians is not to try to fix society immediately through perfect law but to recognise that, in this age of the gospel, lasting transformation begins as Christ rules in hearts through the Holy Spirit. The fruit of the Spirit is love, and so Christians love their neighbours as the good Samaritan did. This means that our energy is not to be restricted to the church community but should also be directed to our society, including the public square. Such love will include contribution to good law reform. As each situation requires, loving contribution brings a range of reasoned arguments, debates, and winsome campaigns, behind the scenes or in public, to promote the public good through effective and attractive persuasion.

Christians bring hope to the world by loving their neighbours. They do so both by sharing the good news and by doing good works as citizens – taking care to imitate Christ's example of courageous love. Within this framework each of us has different callings to emphasise different things, and we should all support one another and use godly wisdom, case by case. And so we come full circle – we are called to love just as God himself has first loved us.

Where to go from here?

This book does not seek to bring anything theologically 'new' other than to co-ordinate familiar and orthodox Bible teaching into a useable framework for Christians involved in the public square. Since it represents the positions of mainstream Bible-believing scholars, the aim is that it can be adopted without controversy by Christians or organisations looking to work together from a shared biblical vision. Here are three suggested routes of application and further work which might be explored as a result of this framework:

1. Structured biblical policies

Christian organisations contributing to the public square might share this framework as a recognised orthodox starting point to make clear to one another and to churches how the Bible shapes and informs their overall policy. For example, an organisation such as the Lawyers' Christian Fellowship could use this framework as *Tier 1* of a three-tier cascade of legal policy resources. *Tier 2* papers could then be prepared on more specific aspects of the public good – such as "The Public Good of Marriage", or "The Public Good of Access to Justice." Each of these generic papers might then flow into more practical *Tier 3* projects – such as legal analysis and evaluation of specific draft legislation. Each tier of the cascade flows directly from this biblical framework but becomes increasingly practical. The further down the cascade, the less likely it is that specific conclusions will find universal agreement. But by tracing the argument from the first tier, and keeping the steps distinct, we can identify points of divergence and still retain fellowship on matters above that point, and, if possible, help one another where there are disagreements.

2. Breadth of Christian engagement

The framework also suggests that the love of the Christian community should seek to contribute to society across the board – not only in relation to some narrow topics or issues. The public good is an integrated whole. Although each individual Christian and organisation will have its own unique gifts and contribution – and limited resources need to be prioritised – this framework suggests that the Christian community as a whole should be interested in supporting the God-given task of civil government as a whole, and looking to co-ordinate together to that end where possible. The prioritisation of resources will often rightly be determined by a focus on policies with the most structural impact on society; but this should not be allowed to detract from the breadth of God's care for all areas of life, and the important way in which this fact complements the gospel.

3. Protecting the gospel's reputation

Christian behaviour should be so obviously 'good' that it will embarrass anyone who tries to damage the gospel's reputation (1 Peter 2:12-20; 3:13-16). Our political work should not undermine the gospel message, nor be confused with it, but should rather complement it. This means we should be alert to minimise possible misunderstandings, and the following considerations may be relevant to Christian organisations operating within contexts which are increasingly secular.

Secular misunderstandings

Selfish moralism. Political authority is often associated with the selfish use of it, and religion is often associated with legalism (chapter 1). Therefore Christian political activity is likely to face the presumption that it is self-serving and moralistic. In an increasingly secular culture, Christian organisations cannot presume on public goodwill. Unlike vibrant churches, they also do not have the 'public relations' advantage of a visible local congregation whose practical love marks us out as an attractive alternative community displaying Christ (John 13:35).

Narrow interests. Life is often fragmented, especially in the West. But all things were created in, through and for Christ (Col. 1:15-20). The Bible presents a comprehensive vision of the creation 'good' (chapter 3). Where Christians, often for good reason, choose to prioritise only some policy areas, this decision might be taken to imply that Christianity itself cares only about those issues, and hence that these must be 'our' issues. This in turn could easily be taken to mean that we are chiefly concerned for ourselves and that our God is not the Lord over all things, people and places. Again, this danger is felt more acutely by Christian policy organisations than by churches or individuals. This is because churches can and should pray for all matters concerning society (1 Tim 2:1-2) and yet they are not responsible to develop particular policies. Conversely, no individual – whether Christian or otherwise – would be expected to have the capacity to become engaged in every area of political policy. But the danger of misunderstanding is greater wherever a policy organisation defines its brand more by its Christianity than by its ongoing policy priorities.

External solutions. A Christian organisation's work in a particular policy area may be taken, wrongly, to represent the totality of Christianity's contribution to that area of human experience. This happens because our work is often interpreted by the world through its own secular categories. So a secular analysis of a political problem might see it in purely human terms and suggest a package of political measures as the solution. In contrast, a comprehensive Christian analysis may indeed include policy measures, but it also sees the spiritual dimension to the problem – and the hope of the Holy Spirit transforming hearts and lives by people being born again (chapter 4). However, to be user-friendly and loving, a 'Christian policy group' may choose to frame its policy recommendations for the public authorities in the more limited terms of the authorities' God-given mandate. The resulting 'Christian policy analysis' then becomes comparatively narrower in scope than the whole 'Christian analysis'. This distinction is almost certainly lost on the average secular observer who assumes that what the Christian group suggests is what Christianity offers. Consequently, when observers look to such an organisation for a Christian answer to national problems, mere *law* can be assumed to be the Christian *gospel*, and Christ is then dishonoured.

Christian responses

To minimise these misunderstandings, our task is to distinguish between the comprehensive message of the gospel and the more limited mandate of public authority. In so doing, our priority is to follow God's lead in distinguishing between the institutions he has established to carry these respective 'swords': church and state. Between those institutional poles lie two dangers, highlighted in chapters 1 and 4. First, it is important that churches should not become (or be seen to become) the arms of political parties. Second, Christian policy organisations should not be confused with church communities, nor their policy recommendations with the gospel and its much more radical message of repentance, faith and eternity.

The Christian gospel tells of the inwardly transforming, eternally saving, and comprehensively restorative kingship of the exalted and returning Lord Jesus Christ as the judge and hope of all creation. Where the gospel message is not explicitly interwoven within our regular public recommendations, we should consider carefully whether or not it is helpful for an organisation to act in the name of Christianity in the public square.

For some of us, the choice might be to continue making public-facing political recommendations but without the gospel message being explicitly integrated within them. If so, we should consider no longer representing our organisation as 'Christian'. Our biblical promotion of the public good could be continued more effectively through a vehicle which is policy-defined and designated accordingly. This leaves less room for the misunderstanding that civil law is the Christian gospel (see above). It is more likely to create opportunities for working effectively with non-Christian groups, donors or governments who share the same limited and defined policy aims. This route focuses on serving the public authority directly within the terms of its limited God-given mandate.

For others, the choice might be to retain a 'Christian' designation but with our practical policy thinking framed explicitly in the context of the message of Christ and the necessity of voluntary Christian conversion for the long-term transformation of society.

It would also allow our strategy and priorities to be traced theologically. This route makes it easier to prioritise serving churches and supporting their mandate (provided we do not trespass into their role). We might use our specialisms to assist churches' public prophetic witness, including their sharp critique of secular society and the urgent call to repentance. We can also assist churches' role behind the scenes – in resourcing, training, networking and equipping Christians for a transformative life in God's world. Believers may then go into the public square better equipped to serve in whatever capacity God has called each one – whether as citizens, lawyers, civil servants or ministers.

Between these two options there is undoubtedly a spectrum along which each organisation will position itself for effective service. Where an organisation chooses to adopt a 'Christian' designation as well as a role of detailed and effective public campaigning, the stakes are much higher. On the one hand, unless the nation is experiencing a wholesale review of its corporate identity, it might well be that the public authority finds it easier to receive policy recommendations without the relevant public good being misinterpreted as being part of the exclusive claim of Christianity. On the other hand, while a Christian message is more likely to be heard on a national scale if it is being introduced as part of detailed political controversy, this approach also introduces many greater risks that the gospel itself will be misunderstood in the ways that we have outlined above. These risks might still be reduced to some extent, however. For example, controversial activity on issues which are likely to be perceived as moralistic could be pursued in deliberate parallel with high profile work on other obvious policy needs where the secular mind has less difficulty in recognising that our motivation and message are sincere love.

Whatever our deployment, we should seek to recognise and support one another's callings generously, and follow Christ as our pattern of effective public love: first to God, and thereby to neighbour (chapter 4). When we prioritise serving God we learn that he has already appointed his own primary servants – giving the civil sword to the public authorities, and giving the sword of the Spirit to the churches. This frees our own organisations to sit comfortably with a secondary and more limited role, serving God best by serving these his servants. In this way even our organisational identity and strategy can adorn the gospel of Christ's kingdom.

> Jesus called them to him and said, "You know that the rulers of the Gentiles lord it over them, and their great ones exercise authority over them. It shall not be so among you. But whoever would be great among you must be your servant, and whoever would be first among you must be your slave, even as the Son of Man came not to be served but to serve, and to give his life as a ransom for many." (Matthew 20:25-28)

When all is said and done – our mandate is clear. As Christians we should love God and love our neighbour. Where the public square is concerned, we have no excuse to hold back, or just do our own thing, or think that evangelism alone is sufficient. We should get involved. Because God first loved us, we too should serve others through *practical love, shaped by the gospel, wisely deployed.* This is good for everyone and it promotes the spread of the good news of the Lord Jesus – who gave his own life as a ransom for many.

PROLOGUE

Beauty on the mountains

If you visit the remote mountains of southern Chin, Myanmar (also known as Burma), you will see that women over the age of fifty have dark marks on their faces. These are said to have originated in the response of ordinary people to a certain kind of political authority.

Hundreds of years ago their region was dangerously close to the kings of the Burmese, the majority tribe who controlled the whole country. The Burmese kings would pass through the local regions and forcibly take the daughters of the Chin people as wives for themselves and their famed harems. Of course, they may not have kept the girls for long and might simply have discarded them. But the girls' families dared not oppose the kings, lest the whole community should suffer.

Eventually these communities vowed their homes and their daughters would never be molested by the Burmese kings again. But their options were limited: they were a minority tribe in a landlocked region. So the action they took in their desperation was shocking. They took their young daughters – between eight and fourteen – and they made sure that no one would find them beautiful enough to steal.

They wrapped their daughters in mats and tied them down showing just their faces. They took leaves from the forest and beat them into a dark fluid. Next they took long strong thorns from the rattan tree and pierced the girls' faces so that they started bleeding. They then inserted the black dye into their cheeks, forehead, chin, even eyelids. It would take from morning until night and it was exceedingly painful. Effectively it was a kind of primitive tattooing designed to make the girl ugly. About a month afterwards her face would stop swelling, and about two months later it would be fully healed. Many girls died from infection. For those who survived, the marks on their faces could never be erased.

The practice worked. Their daughters were not bothered by the kings anymore, and the communities were left unmolested. Their safety had cost them their beauty. But safety it was, and this practice continued for hundreds of years.

Government and gospel

British rule came to Burma in the nineteenth century, and with it came a very different approach to law. As a result, local rulers no longer stole the daughters of nearby tribes. For the first time in hundreds of years, the minority tribe was safe from the molestation of the majority.

But what happened to the practice of tattooing? Even though the danger had been removed, the people continued to subject their daughters to this painful and dangerous process. It even became an art form. The girls grew up to subject their own daughters to the community tradition.

The practice continued until the 1950s when the gospel finally reached this remote part of Chin. In the early nineteenth century the first missionaries like Adoniram Judson had been imprisoned by the anti-Christian Burmese rulers and were unable to preach. Eventually, however, through British influence, missionaries were given freedom to bring the gospel to the Burmese. The gospel passed among the tribes, and was finally carried, after over a hundred years, to arrive at this very remote and mountainous part of Chin.

How beautiful upon the mountains
    are the feet of him who brings good news
Who publishes peace, who brings good news of happiness,
    who publishes salvation, who says to Zion:
"Your God reigns!" (Isaiah 52:7)

When the gospel arrived it spread rapidly and the majority turned to the Lord. Then the people saw that what they were doing to their daughters was evil. The will of the majority in the village was not sufficient reason to inflict pain and mortal danger on the girls, even though they had been doing so for generations. After hundreds of years they stopped the traditional practice. And even the minority who didn't become Christians recognised that the Christian position was the right thing, and they also ended the practice. Their natural beauty returned.

Rather than being forcibly tattooed, Chin children were sent to the Christian schools which became established in the region, and it was reputed to have become one of the best educated areas in Burma.

Military dictatorship

In the 1960s a Burman military dictatorship took control of Burma. For them, Christianity was a threat. And the military was very unhappy that civil servants would send their children to Christian schools for the best education available. So Christian schools were closed down, and Christians began to suffer as a small minority concentrated in certain regions such as Chin. The result was that education regressed to the way it was before and schools in this region reached a very low point.

And this was not the only regression. There is a final sting to this sad tale. Government officials have again primarily come from the majority Burman tribe, and have again been doing as the old kings did – just more subtly. Military officials will pass through an area and see a beautiful woman. They can order the local mayor to arrange for the woman to be brought to them. The mayor will face significant difficulty if he doesn't deliver. And the family of the girl will be in danger themselves if they try to resist. And so Myanmar has come full circle – once again it is dangerous to be the family of a beautiful girl, and people live in fear of the authorities.[7]

But it hasn't quite come full circle, because now the Chin people are Christians. They have changed hearts and new ways of thinking. They are now trusting in God to protect their families and they will not go back to their old practices of tattooing. Instead they are praying for their enemies, that God would forgive them and that this kind of repression would be replaced with good government, so that people will no longer live in fear and darkness.

We can make a few observations from this story:

1. *Political authority is powerful.* It can do great harm when rule exists for the rulers' benefit. Equally, it can protect people from harm when society is ordered by law.

2. *Political authority has a limited ability to change a people for good.* Although law had been brought, it was the spread of the gospel which ultimately brought the culture of tattooing to an end.

3. *People's eternal welfare and their temporal welfare are interrelated in a complex way.* The gospel came through good law which set free missionaries and their message. But law did not change the hearts of the community to rescue the girls' beauty. Only the gospel did that. And in turn the gospel brought education even to the future civil servants. But the hatred of the gospel was interconnected with a desire to hold political power. And the on-going faithfulness of the persecuted Christians may well be used in God's providence to overcome unlawful and oppressive rule today. Our task is to unpick these threads and to understand their relationship.

INTRODUCTION
Sovereign love

A biblical framework for government grows naturally from two simple realities about God.

The love of God

In love God created us as embodied persons who are also social and civil beings. We live in relation to God with air in our lungs, rain on our fields, and orderly relationships with the world and with one another. Since he created us in our totality, he *cares* for us in our totality.

Even if God's only concern was to love people 'spiritually', he would be required nonetheless to keep us alive physically with sufficient peace to restrain us all from killing each other so we could carry, hear and respond to the gospel. Yet it is a dualistic view of God's protection of physical life to see it merely as a means to a 'spiritual' end. God does not take a dismissive view of his creation's physicality: we are his design, and his beauty is reflected physically too. Nor does God's temporal care protect only those who will respond positively to the gospel. He loves his enemies and gives rain to the just and the unjust.

So the love of God is the spring of his 'common grace' for all human life. God's love for humanity points toward some universal loving provision for human civil needs. God's love is good news for the public square.

The sovereignty of God

Our second foundation is God's sovereignty. He is sovereign over creation and over the development of history. The Psalmist exults: "Our God is in the heavens; he does all that he pleases." (Ps. 115:3). He is all powerful and all knowing. "Your God reigns!"

Since God is sovereign we can be sure that his loving provision for civil needs will be coherent with his provision for our eternal needs. He is not like a sprawling bureaucracy with multiple departments working in ignorance against one another.

So the civil sphere and the gospel are not intrinsically opposed to one another. They do not inevitably trip each other up, where devotion to the one necessitates the betrayal of the other. Both are the fruit of God's carefully ordered love for humanity. On the contrary, as a general statement we should expect that where the civil sphere moves toward its God-given design (whatever that may be), the circumstances for the spread of the gospel will, God-willing, be improved. Vice versa, when the gospel is spreading, there should be a knock-on benefit for civil society. This is a virtuous circle emanating from God's sovereign love for humanity.

Of course, there are exceptions which prove the rule. God's sovereignty ensures that when the civil sphere acts against his design, he can nonetheless bring about much good for the gospel. One need only look at the crucifixion of Christ to see how our sovereign God frustrates the plans of his enemies in authority. But we are not to test God by seeking the prosperity of his enemies and their persecutions in order somehow to provoke God's overriding sovereignty. Rather we are to pray that God's will be done on earth as it is in heaven. The fact that God's sovereignty will harness even his enemies for his own purposes is merely further proof of his sovereignty, and so it should point us back to the coherence of his original design. We are better off working with God's sovereignty as its friend than its enemy.

1. PUBLIC AUTHORITY

'God's servant for your *good*'

If God is love and humans have civil needs, we should not be surprised to find that God has instituted public authority.

> "For there is no authority except from God, and the authorities that exist have been instituted by God. ... he is God's servant for your good." (Rom. 13:1, 4)

Public authority is appointed to love

Public authority exists for the good of the people. This sounds odd to the modern ear. Authority is a difficult concept for Western culture today. For Rousseau, authority was in essence a corrupter of humanity – an instrument of corruption, not a weapon against it. Or today we may feel that authority is amoral: it is simply an exercise of power in the interests of the ruler. This is not a new idea. Plato recorded it among the fifth-century BC Greek sophists, for whom justice considered as a question of right was non-existent. Authority is seen as power to be used for our own benefit regardless of whether it is dressed up in the public interest. Or we may feel an instinctive fear of authority because of its connotations of coercion.

Nonetheless, God has provided public authority for our good. Or, if you prefer Augustine's term, the magistrate is there to "love" his people. In the *City of God* (14.28) Augustine contrasts the two ways humanity can operate: in the spirit of the earthly city or the heavenly city. In this passage Augustine describes two contrasting approaches to political authority:

We see then that the two cities were created by two kinds of love: the earthly city was created by self-love reaching the point of contempt for God, the Heavenly City by the love of God carried as far as contempt of self. In fact, the earthly city glories in itself, the Heavenly City glories in the Lord. The former looks for glory from men, the latter finds its highest glory in God. ... In the former, the lust for domination lords it over princes as over the nations it subjugates; in the other both those put in authority and those subject to them serve one another in love, the rulers by their counsel, the subjects by obedience. The one city loves its own strength shown in its powerful leaders; the other says to its God: "I will love you, my Lord, my strength." [8]

As Mike Ovey commented:

Augustine thinks that a ruler can have authority *and* love his or her people, and thinks that a subject can love his or her ruler. And in response to the dichotomy between authority and love that we instinctively feel in our cynical world – Augustine says: 'No. It should not be so, not among you: "Do not lord it as the Gentiles do."' ... We are being told that there is authority and that there is love and that the two can go together.

'Love' may sound out of place in the context of contemporary political theory. But in the context of the sovereign love of God who has ordained both the spreading gospel and the public authority, it is of no surprise at all that God's authority and love should find continuation in the love of the public authority for the people. Jesus says the summary of the law is to love, and this is quoted later in Romans 13 itself, as a natural part of Paul's wider argument from chapter 12 about the life of love.

Public authority is instituted by God. So the proper context for civil government is love for society. Love for society seeks the good of society. Thinking back to our Prologue, love does not steal your daughter or cause minorities to live in fear.

Love – with authority to commend good and punish evil

If both rulers and citizens should act in love, how are they distinguished? What identifies a public authority?

Rulers have authority to punish those who do evil and commend those who do good (Rom. 13:3-4). The very same terms are repeated in 1 Peter 2:14: the ruler is there "to praise those who do good and to punish those who do evil." These two descriptions by two different apostles repeat the same core mandate for the way in which God has instituted public authority to benefit society.

In other words, rulers have authority from God to exercise good judgment in relation to other people. This is not merely to distinguish those doing good from those doing evil, but to execute justice on behalf of God using "the sword".

> "…for he is God's servant for your good. But if you do wrong, be afraid, for he does not bear the sword in vain. For he is the servant of God, an avenger who carries out God's wrath on the wrongdoer." (Rom. 13:4)

But are we still in the realm of 'love'? Isn't it self-contradictory to continue to speak of love in the spheres of judgment and morality? Some seek to prioritise love and so abandon judgment and morality; others prioritise judgment and morality and forget love. Can these be reconciled?

Love and judgment

Can love execute *judgment*? This very question was posed in Cranmer's first book of homilies (1547), in the sixth homily, on Christian love and charity. The homily provides the answer. Love has two offices:

> The one office of charity is, to cherish good and harmless men, not to oppress them with false accusations, but to encourage them with rewards to do well, … defending them with the sword from their adversaries. … The other office of

charity is, to rebuke, correct and punish vice, without regard
of persons, and is to be used against them only that be evil
men, and malefactors or evil doers. And that it is as well the
office of charity to rebuke, punish and correct them that be
evil, as it is to cherish and reward them that be good and
harmless. [9]

Love *must* execute judgment. It is impossible to love our children
unless we protect them from harm, and correct them from harm-
ing themselves. So, in relation to the magistrate and evildoers, the
homily continues, love's duty is "to procure and seek their correction and due punishment, that they may thereby either be brought
to goodness, or at the least that God and the commonwealth be less
hurt and offended."

So we note that the authority is called to love society *corporately*,
within which – rather than contrary to which – it acts in love towards the individual offender. Hence the homily states the hope
that the offender will be brought to goodness. However, 'the commonwealth' is the priority: it is blessed by the offender's reform or
otherwise by his restraint or removal. By the same corporate love
the sword protects the commonwealth from corporate threats such
as invasion and civil insurrection. It would be unloving to abandon
love's sword. Those who see a fundamental conflict between love
and judgment perhaps neglect love's duty to society corporately in
favour of a kind of love to the individual offender. In an age of in-
dividualism this is a common move – where individual rights may
eclipse the blessing of public order.

Public order *per se* is not the goal: as if the mere dominance of a
military dictatorship would suffice. On the contrary, we pray for
public authorities: "…that we may lead a peaceful and quiet life,
godly and dignified in every way." (1 Tim 2:2). Love's sword provides *such* a public order that will *benefit* the public: one where evil
is punished and good is promoted, where there is peaceful space for
godly and dignified lives.

Love and morality

But is *love* really concerned with morality? What do we make of these unavoidable references in the biblical texts to 'good' and 'evil'? Isn't morality repugnant in the public square? Further, doesn't talk about public morality undermine Christianity's emphasis on grace and the gospel?

The solution is found in the difference between moralism and the moral order of the universe. When referring to 'morality' we must be sure which of these we are talking about, and bear in mind that today's world knows everything about the former, and almost nothing of the latter.

Moralism aims at moral behaviour for its earthly goal. Its motivation is human pride – to earn favour with God or simply to achieve outward conformity to certain moral standards. In relation to God, moralism is associated with a denial of the good news of Christ: it requires moral effort to please God rather than the free acceptance of Christ's life and death on our behalf. In relation to society it has become associated with hypocrisy and the failure to distinguish between 'crime' and 'sin'. It is criticised for requiring non-Christians to behave like Christians through criminalising as many sins as possible. Moralism in the public authority will use the sword – coercive means – to achieve this end. Yet this follows naturally from its aim for outward moral behaviour *per se*. This is the way of the 'earthly city', and it is a shame when Christians represent it.

The moral order, on the other hand, is the Creator's loving ordering of the universe so that all his creatures have the freedom to be what they were created to be. It is an objective 'design language' which enables the creation to function and thrive. It is called a 'moral' order because its ordering reflects the order of God who created the world not as an arbitrary sphere but as a consistent communication of his own character and nature. Therefore as the source and pattern of life, God is at the same time the definition of what is right *and* what is good for what he has made. Consequently goodness and morality are the two sides of the same coin: what is right and moral will be best for us. What is best for us will be what is right for us, but when we reject God we simultaneously reject life. That is why when as humans we kill those created in God's image we not only sin but we harm ourselves; and when we protect the weak we reflect God's nature and benefit our own families and future.

The distinction between moralism and the moral order is *essential* for our discussion, yet it does little more than follow Augustine's distinction between the two cities. While moralism aims at morality itself ultimately for human pride, God's common grace ensures that creation's moral order provides morality *for our benefit* – for the enjoyment of God's gift of life. This moral order can (and should) be utilised by the public authority for the benefit of society. This is the chief basis of Romans 13:1-7 and its place within Paul's argument. While the section contains moral language and clearly operates within the moral order, the *aim* of the public authority is not morality *per se* but benefit. Paul's appeal is that "he is God's servant for *your* good" (emphasis added) and so Christians have no need to avenge themselves. We shouldn't resent paying taxes but should honour and submit to the authorities and continue a life of love ourselves.

Love – with authority limited for public action

Public order not private life

Behind people's fear of moralism stands a fear of unlimited 'public' authority intervening in every aspect of the 'private' life. When morality in itself becomes the goal of the authority, the authority should, logically, concern itself with the whole of the moral order. No part of the universe lies beyond the ambitions of its sword. There would be just as much need to punish those who *think* wrong as those who *do* wrong – all thought and speech should be corrected, not just action.

But Romans 13 shows the concern of the authority is the public action of those who do good and those who do evil. We are able to distinguish between sins and crimes because the task of public authority is not morality itself but the beneficial structure of *public order* according with (but not co-extensive with) the moral order.

Sins transgress the moral order of the universe. But, rightly understood, crimes are only those sins which directly attack the public order of society.

The public authority is thus concerned not with private matters but public. What does this mean? Almost all speech and action affects other people in some way. So when we say the public authority is to protect public order we do not mean all matters of the creation order (or, if you prefer, the moral order) which affect other people, but in essence only those matters which affect other people *structurally*. We will consider this in more detail in the 'Public Good' chapter. For now, the public order is like the skeleton of the "body politic". This is the fundamental God-given structuring upon which the rest of society depends, and any harm to this has an exponentially negative impact on everything else. Crimes are like broken bones rather than merely grazed flesh: if bones don't heal or heal crooked, the rest of the body suffers. Thus both lying and perjury are morally equivalent in relation to God's character of truth – but this equivalence is not the concern of the public authority. What matters is simply the impact on public order: what will harm society structurally? So, of the two, perjury alone is considered to be a public offence and designated as a crime. Interpersonal lying can usually be left to the transforming power of the gospel.

This public/private distinction is essential for our discussion and follows from the equally essential distinction between moralism and the beneficial moral order. These two principles show that biblical government is concerned with public ordering for society's benefit and everything else we expect from it should sit comfortably under this combined heading.

The state is not the church

The fear of unlimited or intrusive authority also explains much modern reluctance to allow religion into the public square. If moralism alone threatens to intrude in every part of our lives, surely religion will do even worse? Many assume that Christian political involvement ultimately tends toward an intrusive church-state, with the church aspiring to turn all sins into crimes.

But the true gospel is not moralism or even 'religion' in that sense – it is the good news of the Lord Jesus Christ. True Christianity rejects a church-dominated state. On the contrary, it provides better a limitation to the dominance of state authority than we see in many nations today. We can see this in two ways.

Negatively, God has not ordained a church-state on this side of Christ's return. From his unique position of having 'all authority' God has sovereignly established church and state as *different institutions* defined by different *mandates*. As an institution the church has been given the great commission to preach the gospel – a rational message of information to bring. Its activity facing the world is to be directed to that end: it bears the sword of the Spirit which reaches hearts internally. The glory of Christ's good news inspires voluntary faith and brings sincere worship. Jesus doesn't need faith to be compelled but has commissioned his message to be broadcast. Conversely, as an institution, civil government has been given the mandate to do justice by law. Its discussions and judgments are to be embodied in effective outward action: it bears the external sword of justice. Each institution has delegated authority from God with a defined mandate, and each complements the other. They are plural because they are separated by God and each is accountable to God.

This distinction is possible because the church as an *institution* is not the sum of the Christian life for its members. For most of the time, Christians live and take part in society as members of other bodies: as family members, as employees, as citizens. We can describe Christians in this way as the organic church within the world. Thus the gospel taught by full-time church ministers should move regular church members into practical action as citizens. The Christian life is not lived only within the four walls of the church but also within the four sides of the public square. If any church claims to preach the gospel but its members do not live out the implications of their faith by acting for the good of others, then it is possibly not preaching the gospel: the Bible says that faith is shown by works. Thus, where gospel-loving church members not only serve within society but also happen to be officers of the public authority, then the good works of their Christian life will contribute to, or even become, the loving action of civil government for the blessing of the world. So in this sense the church organically overlaps with the state, but institutionally they are to be separate.

Thus, *positively*, true Christianity provides a living alternative to the monopoly of state power in society. It provides a gospel message which changes hearts and brings the vibrant impact of local churches in society. It is no accident that, for example, Marxism grew out of an atheistic account where this powerful alternative is absent.

Clear terminology

Two points of confusing terminology can be clarified to help one another. Should we as Christians advocate 'theocracy' or the 'separation of church and state'? Depending on how the terms are understood our aim should be both and neither.

'Theocracy' is commonly understood to mean an institutional identification of church and state – something which the New Testament age does not countenance. This use of the term is often paralleled in some way with some Islamic states, or with the uniquely typological rule of Israel in the Old Testament. However, on the basis of its etymology – it simply reads: 'God's rule'. And it is true it is the rule of God which provides the basis for the human rule in the senses we have just seen: first by his sovereign rule instituting public authority and providing the moral order, separating the state from the church and giving it a coherent mandate and secondly by the rule of his kingdom coming directly through human hearts rather than nation states (see, chapter 4, Public Hope). We should beware that some Christians may try to use the term 'theocracy' in this wider positive sense and we should clarify our use of the term in discussion with each other.

Similarly, the 'separation of church and state' can mean different things to different people. We can affirm the phrase when it refers to an *institutional separation* of church and state, for reasons we have outlined: God has separated them by giving them different roles, and the officers of one are not thereby officers of the other. However, many secularists use the term to mean that there is a *philosophical separation* between public life and religious thought – that religion is inherently private and its contributions are by definition inaccessible and untestable and should be screened from public life. We disagree because we believe that all of reality comes from God. This means public life concerns him and our policy contributions can be made in creational terms which are accessible to everyone. Finally, radical secularists may even use the phrase to mean there should be a kind of personnel *segregation* of church and state – where individual Christians themselves are automatically deemed unsuitable for involvement in state affairs. Again, this study seeks to demonstrate the opposite.

We need to take time and be generous with one another as we clarify our terms, and not rush to conclusions. Christian thinking and contribution to the public square has not always been clear on these matters.

Love rules according to law

We can now step back from the detail and recognise the picture of public authority which our study has presented. Putting it together, the public authority rightly rules according to *law*.

Thus we have the essentials of the Bible's description of the rule of law: a tag which can today sound increasingly thin. To summarise, it is not sufficient to say that a government has authority, or even that it uses its authority to sustain a consistent public order. This public order should be for our *good*: it should accord with the moral order of creation to the benefit of society. Such law is not arbitrary or amoral but begins to be accessible to everyone (not least because God has placed law in all human hearts through our conscience – as we shall explore in the next chapter). Further, this authority must be defined and limited in its reach, confining itself to the public structuring of society and not intervening in the God-given freedoms of people's lives.

This rule of law is precious. As the Roman Empire declined in the West in AD 410, Augustine asked: "What is the difference between the rightful authority and a band of brigands?" He answered, "Law and justice." In the same way, the Renaissance Italian writer Salutati (1331-1406) brought a similar conclusion, observing: "The special quality of the tyrant is that he does not rule according to law." [10]

Rule is distinct from law and should be subject to it. The distinction is possible because law comes from God and not from rulers: public authority is instituted by God with a mandate from God to rule in accordance with his ordering of creation. So we can echo John of Salisbury who wrote (in his book *Policraticus* c.1159) that the central criterion for tyranny – whether in the context of civil, ecclesiastical or family authority – is "a repudiation of God's law". [11]

As Mike Ovey noted:

> In answer to the kind of charge that 'we don't want to have a monarchical conception of God', John of Salisbury is telling us that it is precisely the fact that we think all authority comes from God the King that actually renders people accountable for it. He would even go so far as to say that there are remedies against abuse.

Thus all exercise of authority is accountable. The whole book of Daniel makes the case for divine accountability. Nebuchadnezzar and Belshazzar are weighed and humbled by *God*. What about us? Should our honour for authority's throne inspire opposition to the tyrant sitting upon it? Mike Ovey pointed out that Thomas Aquinas (1225-1274) saw force as legitimate against a tyrant (in *Summa Theologiae* II-II.42.2): resisting the tyrant is not sedition, but a defence of justice.[12] John of Salisbury argued further that *fatal force* was legitimate.[13] Later on, although the Council of Constance (1415, Session XV) repudiated the *assassination* of a tyrant, the Council retained the essential analytical tool by which a tyrant was to be identified.

Whatever our view on sanctions, the rule/law distinction allows us to detect tyranny at a much earlier stage than if we had only a stark alternative between oppressive rule and the lack of rule – as if tyranny is no more than the opposite of anarchy. The reality is more nuanced because at all times the ruler must act in accordance with law. Here is Salutati again:

> We conclude, therefore, that a tyrant is either one who usurps a government, having no legal title for his rule, or one who governs autocratically or rules unjustly or does not observe laws or equity... (*De Tyranno* 1)

There is a tyranny of lawlessness as well as a tyranny of oppressive law – as the Greek city states discovered in the fifth and sixth centuries BC. Incoming rulers claimed to set people free but were then found to allow evil to flourish: tyrannical rule gives its followers 'freedom' to kidnap and rape people because they are their friends.

Mike Ovey pointed out an important implication of this analysis:

> As we talk about the concept of tyranny, which is such a central one for public authority, as we look as Christian tradition, we realise that *tyrants are fundamentally anti-law*.

> But cannot a modern state be a tyrant in both ways – both by the oppressiveness of its regimentation and legislation in that very traditional sense, but also in the way that it is capable of colluding in wickedness? Such a state, of course, has come to be the complete *reverse* of the Romans 13 state: oppressing the good and facilitating the wicked.

Conclusion

The core mandate of the public authority is to rule according to law. Such rule may spring from a variety of reasons and with more or less understanding. It seems broadly recognisable to everyone, and many across the world can aspire to it. But on the other hand, we have seen that limited human authority only stands consistently within the comprehensive authority of God – and his rule is proclaimed as part of the gospel message.

The poetry of Job 28 suggests a similarly nuanced account of human wisdom. We can use human skill for many fine endeavours and even bring gold out of the earth (which was one of the most striking technological accomplishments of Job's era, sitting as it did on the cusp between the Bronze and the Iron Age). But we can't use even that gold to buy God's wisdom – the treasures of which are found only in Christ and his plan for creation.

For Mike Ovey, our conclusion should reflect something of a tension:

> Job 28 tells you on the one hand about human *abilities* in terms of common grace but it also tells you about human *inability*. It leads me to think that, as I read and as I follow through non-Christian writers and thinkers, there may be things that by common grace they grasp in one way or another – a wisdom under the sun – that has a place, and with which we may talk.

> But it also tells me of the utter incompleteness of the kind of wisdom that is being offered without partnership and (dare I say it) guidance from those who know the wisdom of the Creator directly from what he has said. The thing that strikes me is the desperate need that the public square has for an authentically Christian voice, precisely because, wonderful though common grace is, the wisdom that it offers is so radically incomplete.

To reflect something of this balance, each chapter concludes with key points structured to reflect the distinction between the action required from the public authority and the comprehensive wisdom of the gospel message.

CHAPTER SUMMARY

1. Public Authority – 'God's servant for your *good*'

The **government's mandate** is to rule according to law for the good of society.

▷ This means protecting and encouraging those who do good to society, and correcting and restraining those who do it evil, thus maintaining public life in a way which accords with the moral order of creation, including our human design.
▷ This also means public authority is limited and it should not interfere beyond its public sphere. It is not mandated to renew human hearts or minds from within. Instead the rule of law is to protect human freedoms for everyone's benefit.

The **gospel's message** explains this mandate, telling of God's own rule which is the only basis for the rule of law.

▷ Public authority has its legitimate and limited existence because of divine authority. Human rule stands under law which accords with the moral order of God's creation.
▷ Human freedom is God-given and should be protected from 'state salvation' or state oppression, in the knowledge that only Christ's reign can set people's hearts free in a way that public authority can never achieve.

2. PUBLIC TRUTH

How can we *know* what is 'good'?

Loving rule for society depends on knowing what is true about society. Public authority is to rule according to law for our good. But how do we know what is good and evil for society?

Truth is good news

The need for truth

We often pursue what is good for society *without* asking what is true about society. The connection is unfashionable because 'truth' is archaic. Post-modern Western culture no longer believes it is possible to give a unified account of human society. Historical attempts to do so are associated with violence. Society is considered too complex, too diverse, for any single human conception of it. So a claim that something is 'true' for everyone signals arrogance – as if the speaker is not limited by his own perspectives of context and experience. In other words, the subjectivity of knowledge implies that any such declaration *cannot* be more than a thinly veiled attempt to assert power over another person. 'Public truth' is perceived as at best unreachable, and at worst aggressively manipulative. In political life today, claims to truth are not seen as good.

Yet our pursuit of a common good is hampered without it. What is the basis for a policy decision now? Variously we choose what has been shown to work, we copy other countries, we choose what is financially expedient, we seek to please special interest groups, and we follow the fashionable mood of the political and media elite. But these can often represent increasingly disparate lines of analysis and can present flagrant contradictions. A policy proposal may

fly in the face of sociological evidence and prove to be economically costly, but may be accepted nonetheless because it is politically
fashionable. And what assumptions determine what it means for a
policy to have been shown to 'work'?

Without some shared intellectual base, political discussions very
easily degenerate. Ironically, they become more or less aggressive
or powerful assertions of one opinion over another. Where policy is
made on this uncertain basis, the resulting laws become uncertain
too. Without a consensus on truth we have no basis for the consistent rule of law. Public good requires public truth.

There is a need for a higher standard of truth and constructive
principled analysis in an age of shouting and the fear of corruption.
Today's public square is searching in the dark for the truth it has
lost. In a diverse world we are looking for a standard around which
to unite and bring lawful order, one which is accessible to everyone,
and which can serve people and not manipulate them. We are looking for a truth which is good.

The revelation of truth

There is good news for the public square. According to John's
Gospel:

> In the beginning was the Word, and the Word was with God,
> and the Word was God. He was in the beginning with God.
> All things were made through Him, and without Him noth-
> ing was made that was made. In Him was life, and the life
> was the light of men. And the light shines in the darkness,
> and the darkness did not comprehend it. ... And the Word
> became flesh and dwelt among us, and we beheld His glory,
> the glory as of the only begotten of the Father, full of grace
> and truth. (John 1:1-4, 14, NKJV)

Enlightenment for all spheres of human life is rooted in the life of
Christ. There is revelation in the life of his creation and incarnation:
there is truth in his goodness. Christ is the one who declared: "I am
the way and the truth and the life" (John 14:6). Because of Christ,

to say that something is 'true' for society can be both good and gracious.

Truth derives from creation

Truth exists as a meaningful public concept because it is objective, rational, communicable and gracious. All four characteristics derive from Christ as the Word, or *logos*, through whom the universe was created and is now sustained. Each is undermined today so it is important to take time to recover these aspects clearly in our own minds.

Truth is objective – law can apply universally

If truth is entirely subjective, created by everyone's own perception of it, then it follows we should have different legal standards for different enthusiasts, families or sub-cultures depending on their own particular view. States break down into tribes unless everyone happens to share the same viewpoint. The alternative is to hold them together by the exercise of dominant power.

But creation shows us truth is not subjective. Reality does not depend on our conception of it, but on how God made it. All things were made through Christ the *logos* as a meaningful communication of God's glory and without our assistance: we do not create reality, but Reality creates us. All humans, regardless of whether they are Christians, are made in God's image, from the same human family, with the same responsibility to represent him in the world and have dominion over the world. We all inhabit the same moral order of the universe which is patterned on the same character of God. So it follows that when we say that truth is *objective*, we mean that it exists independently of ourselves who seek to know it through our subjective minds and opinions. It means that we do not say a principle of public order is "true for me" but not "true for you". There is a good design for humanity which we can seek for everyone's benefit, whether we know it or not, or like it or not.

Truth is rational – we can be a thinking society

Political *thinking* does not come automatically. Arbitrary justice is a common feature of autocratic rule and it also gave us the notorious 'trial by ordeal'. Not every culture in the world has seen intellectual content as fundamental to justice. Today political discussion risks becoming increasingly banal in the search for easily-quoted sound bites, and so arguments themselves become a means of entertainment rather than the pursuit of a conclusion.

But because Christ is the *logos*, the consistent 'format' of reality is *rational*: Sense made it and so it makes sense. Both the objects we study (e.g. social factors) and the subjects who study them (us), share the same God-given format. This coherence makes it possible for us to understand the world around us. Therefore regardless of a person's faith position, it is valid and meaningful for humans to examine and understand reality – to reason – to pursue truth. Here we have a base for political rationality.

Today, many of those who prize political rationality despise religious contribution to public debate. But the rational public square should welcome authentic Christian engagement. Since Christ is the *logos*, and reality is rational, then people studying the public square *as it really is* are engaging in both political and Christian activity at the same time. Properly understood, both Christianity and politics operate in accordance with reason, and neither should exclude the other as if they operate upon mutually exclusive principles. As David McIlroy pointed out:

> It is Kant who really gives us the idea that life divides into two compartments: a public compartment where we discuss things with one another on the basis of reason and a private compartment where reason has nothing to say. It is Kant who establishes the modern trade-off regarding religion: no religion will be subjected to question on the grounds of its rationality provided that religions stay out of the public square. [14]

Christ's creation denies this reason/religion dichotomy. So when we seek to know public truth we are not self-consciously ruling out religious thought in pursuit of something more rational. And nor is Christian thought the source of arbitrary requirements which are detrimental to a non-Christian society. All truth is God's truth, and his design principles for the world are accessible to everyone.

Truth is communicable – we prize discourse not violence

Leaders *parley* in Parliament, and rightly so. But this does not happen by itself. In many contexts it is difficult to bring leaders around a table to generate political solutions: what is the point of talking when we all see things differently?

But through Christ reality is objective and rational and so public truth is communicable truth. We can meaningfully talk to one another about what is good for society. And because we all share the same reality deriving from Christ in whose image we are made, we do not each perceive an arbitrary world through utterly independent filters. We are born into the same family of reality and all naturally speak its common language. With careful communication two people *can* be sure they are both talking about the same thing. Communication is not pointless but constructive.

Truth is good – we can serve one another

Truth makes love possible. By discussing *my truth* I am at once discussing *your truth*, because all truth is *our truth* by the gift of God. Of course we must all benefit from one another's perspectives on the same truth. But because truth is reconciled to itself, a shared discussion of truth, even persuasion itself, is in essence an act of reconciliation rather than aggression.

Truth affirms the *diversity* of the world and so allows us to protect the weak. Because we can understand the common, objective framework within which we all operate, we are better equipped to recognise, appreciate and protect the diversity God has created within its unity. We can allow everyone to be who they are created to be within the world God has made. This diversity reflects God's own infinite and many-sided glory.

When, on the contrary, 'truth' becomes the creation and reflection of each individual finite mind, it cannot adequately conceive of God's diversity and indeed produces a much less diverse and less unified conception of reality. In the context of the public square, this results in political power being used only in the service of the private 'truth' created by each ruler or party in its own image and for its own interests. Diversity is then maintained only at the expense of a unified political doctrine. But without a unified political doctrine it is difficult to maintain the unity of public order. We can see-saw between public order and disunity without ever appreciating diversity. Diversity then exists merely as the multiplicity of miniature and competing unities, and inevitably the weak and marginalised remain so – and at increasing risk of oppression.

Therefore, because of Christ and his role in creation, public truth exists, and it is good. But how is it accessed?

Truth is revealed in creation

Public truth provides the basis for *natural law* theories. Here, society's best interests are identified in accordance with an objective good defined as the natural order. Christians understand this as God's design for his creation, and this coherence explains the strength of natural law theories.

As David McIlroy summarised: "The idea of 'general revelation' points out that what God has revealed of himself and of God's design for human life *through the way the created world works* is consistent with what God has revealed of himself and of God's design for human life *in the Bible and in the person of Jesus.*"

Thus, for natural law theories, public truth exists. In other words, natural law theories find their strength in the question of being, or, 'ontology'.

But how do we know what this natural order actually is? This is the question of knowledge, or, 'epistemology'. Much historical natural law theory has been rationalistic on this point. In a universe which was assumed to be rational, it was not only thought that the laws of physics could be determined rationally but also that the laws applicable to human nature could be determined rationally.

This is where non-Christian natural law reasoning falters. Although God has revealed objective truth in the natural world, this natural revelation isn't easy to interpret. What one generation thinks is perfectly natural – lifelong, monogamous, heterosexual relationships – the next generation thinks is old-fashioned and out of line with its own desires or even with the observation of the animal kingdom.

> Historical study shows that it has been possible to understand under 'order of nature' just about anything a philosopher wanted; Stoicism or Epicureanism, creative evolution or political restorationism, Puritan democracy or Aryan dictatorship.[15]

What is the problem? Didn't we establish that because of *creation*, both the world and we who study it share the same rational format? We can identify three problems in reading the world:

1. *The world we look at is not perfect but fallen.*

To employ David McIlroy's metaphor: when we look at the world around us what we see is a palimpsest. A palimpsest is a piece of parchment or paper which has been used for writing on twice. It was quite common in the days when paper was much rarer than it is today for paper to be re-used, even on the same side, so you would have a piece of paper which had been written on twice. Our world is like a palimpsest. There are two realities which we can see when we look at our world: one is the reality of the world as God's good creation, the other is the reality of the world as fallen, full of sin and violence.

What we see are two pictures, overlaid one on top of the other. One picture is a picture of a good world, created good by God and still displaying much of its beauty. But that picture is obscured by another picture, a picture of the dirt, mess and scars which evil has caused.

So the onus is now on the observer. But another problem follows.

2. We who look at the world are fallen.

Our reasoning is distorted and defective, affected by self-interest, short-sightedness, ignorance and simple error. Thus Romans 1 teaches that although God has revealed himself to human beings, human beings have rejected that revelation: we have suppressed the truth, preferring lies to the truth and injustice to God's moral design for humanity. A rejection of God involves a rejection of God's natural order which reflects him. Paul observed: "...they became futile in their thinking, and their foolish hearts were darkened. Claiming to be wise, they became fools..." (Romans 1:21-22)

The short-sightedness and errors are not just our own but they are also corporate. We do not start with a blank canvas. Our culture interprets the world in a particular way, it has particular flashes of insight and particular blind spots. Cultures can be blind to issues of race, sex, slavery and so forth.

3. We are also finite

Our perspective is limited because we are finite creatures. We do not have a God's eye view of things because we are not God. In other words, there are some things which even perfect observers in a perfect world could not be expected to deduce about their own well-being.

This means that the rationalist idea that everyone who uses logic correctly will look at the same landscape of the world in the same way and reach the same conclusions is fatally flawed.

David McIlroy analysed the position helpfully:

> Rationalism seeks to understand the natural order without reference to Christ. According to a rationalist theory of nat-

ural law, the propositions of natural law are the conclusions which everyone would arrive at if only they were thinking correctly. Rationalism was a product of the Enlightenment, an era which lost sight of the doctrine of the fall. Enlightenment thinkers, overawed by the scientific discoveries about the order of nature, concluded that nature constituted a closed, self-sustaining system whose moral laws could be discerned by the power of human reason just as easily as its physical laws were being uncovered by scientific advances.

Rationalism is under severe strain today as we have realised that there is more to moral disagreement than simply faulty logic. It has been increasingly recognised that people do not reason from a neutral starting point but rather from a particular starting point, arrived at as a result of the parental, social, cultural, historical, religious and other influences which have shaped their worldview. People reasoning from different presuppositions will, or may well, arrive at different conclusions, each of which makes logical sense on its own basis.

Further, if the world is fallen, and humans are fallen and finite, then it is not only rationalism which is flawed, but so is any system or community of truth-discovery whose ingredients include nothing greater than human observation or reflection upon the world. And this is precisely the problem that secular philosophy has encountered.

Truth is revealed in the Bible

Creation and the Bible

Humanity needs this general revelation in nature – grounded in Christ's act of creation – to be clarified and extended by God's special revelation of Christ's incarnation which is recorded in the Bible.

David McIlroy demonstrated how we stand in the tradition of our theological forebears:

The author of *Paradise Lost*, John Milton argued that 'A kind of gleam or glimmering' of the natural law 'remains in the hearts of all mankind' even after the Fall, but that God's revelation is necessary both to make clear to us what the natural law requires and to give us the strength to seek to obey it. Milton rejected purely rationalist theories of natural law, writing 'If there were no God, there would be no real dividing line between right and wrong. What was called virtue, and what vice, would depend upon mere arbitrary opinion.' Christian natural law theory, rightly understood, sees the moral law in creation to be more clearly revealed in the law of Moses and then given full clarification in the teaching of Jesus.

Both Thomas Aquinas[16] and John Calvin[17] taught that the moral law contained within the Mosaic Law reiterates and clarifies the natural law. Building on mediaeval Christian thought, the Calvinist tradition taught that the Ten Commandments were the best summary of the natural law which was imprinted on every human being's conscience and that they were the clearest source of the principles about how to love God, one's neighbour and oneself.

After the fall, it is impossible to propound adequate Christian creation ethics without reference to the example of Israel as God's redeemed nation and to Jesus Christ as God's chosen Redeemer.

The Bible is not merely a private or 'religious' text in today's categories. It is our Creator's message to humanity, including a description of his own creation order and the revelation of public truth. The Bible is consistent with creation. We will not find the Bible contradicting reality but affirming and explaining it. Taking the example of marriage once more, the Bible confirms and clarifies that marriage is the proper and healthy context for sexual relationships and family life, and it also tells us about the roles of husband, wife, parents and children, and their impact on welfare and education.

Similarly, a law today may aim at what is in a person's *best interests*. Because this is a question of God's loving ordering, the Bible will apply to this issue. We should not close the Bible after reading in it that we should "love our neighbour" and then proceed to apply our own cultural presuppositions as to what love means. Rather, we can keep the Bible open and examine what it says about God's good ordering for his creation, and how he has designed us to thrive.

The Bible has been shown in history to provide a solid basis for public truth and the rule of law in the context of its gospel message. It provided a significant role in the origin and development of common law. One might ask how the English political tradition could develop without a written constitution. In a very significant sense it *was* written: in the Bible, which so profoundly shaped the English language and culture.

The Puritan century (from the 1550s to 1660s) had a profound and lasting impact on British culture. It began with the English Bible. It ended with the rule of law, the sovereignty of Parliament, and the first modern constitutional monarchy. In between, scholarly pastor-theologians showed their people the implications of Christ for every area of life – from saving the soul to reforming the public square. It was not just the age of Shakespeare's theatre: large sections of the population were eager to hear frequent biblical preaching.

By popular demand, John Rogers (c. 1570-1636) preached from his Essex church roof every Tuesday at 8:00 am – before market day in Dedham – to the thousand or so gathered to hear him in the square below, no longer fitting in the building. One Cambridge student hired a horse to hear him, and came away deeply moved by the experience of God's word: Thomas Goodwin would go on to became a pastor-theologian and eventually preach to MPs in Parliament. Goodwin entered ministry at the encouragement of Richard Sibbes, the Puritan vicar of Holy Trinity, Cambridge. The "heavenly Doctor Sibbes" held three jobs simultaneously: he was also Master of St Catherine's College, Cambridge and preacher of Gray's Inn, London. It was there he taught lawyers "to study law but practice divinity" and not to advise a client without being first a "client at the throne of Grace". He gave them a biblical worldview including the accountability of kings. One who heard him often was John

Cooke (1608-1660), the brave Christian barrister who would go on not only to prosecute King Charles I and establish tyranny as a crime, but also to originate the 'right to silence', the 'cab rank' rule of advocacy, and the duty to act free of charge for the poor. He was not alone, but represented a Bible-loving professional class within a gospel-affected population.[18]

Over the century, each generation trained the next to apply the Bible to their lives and culture. Not only were people saved and personal holiness encouraged, but the rule of law and professional standards emerged in England without an otherwise written constitution.

But how do we jump from the basic principle – "keep the Bible open" – or even "preach the Bible" to more workable principles of public ethics and modern law today?

Truth begins in the Old Testament

Christ and the Bible

Christ is not only the ground of truth but also its subject and teacher. As teacher, Christ shows us that public truth begins in the Old Testament.

In the words of David McIlroy: "Jesus is our guide to interpreting the rest of the Bible. Beyond the words of Jesus, the New Testament says relatively little about the Christian contribution to society beyond the church and the role of political authorities. What it does say is very important, particularly Romans 13:1-7 which Mike Ovey looked at in the last seminar. Nonetheless, a Christian account of social and political morality built on the New Testament alone would be relatively thin. A fully developed Christian contribution to public life must take adequate account of the Old Testament, because that is what Jesus did."

Jesus relied on the account of creation from the book of Genesis and the Law of Moses as authoritative accounts of human society's true design.

The challenge of the Old Testament

But as soon as we consider the Old Testament as public truth we encounter two apparently opposite concerns. The first is that we often don't like what is *clear* in the Old Testament, and the second is that we often despair of what is *complex* in it. But Christ is the way through both obstacles.

Paul wrote of those who read the Old Testament without an understanding of Christ:

> ...their minds were hardened. For to this day, when they read the old covenant, that same veil remains unlifted, because only through Christ is it taken away. Yes, to this day whenever Moses is read a veil lies over their hearts. But when one turns to the Lord, the veil is removed. Now the Lord is the Spirit, and where the Spirit of the Lord is, there is freedom. And we all, with unveiled face, beholding the glory of the Lord, are being transformed into the same image from one degree of glory to another. For this comes from the Lord who is the Spirit. (2 Cor. 3:14-18)

Christ reconciles us to the clarity of the Old Testament

We often *don't like* what we see clearly in the Old Testament. We find ourselves loving to do what it clearly says is bad for us, and vice versa. It points out that we are hating one another, divorcing, being disobedient to parents, being sexually immoral and taking what belongs to others – and that we can't do anything about it for ourselves. And so we see the Old Testament not as a blessing but as Paul described it, "the ministry of condemnation" (2 Cor. 3:9). No-one likes being condemned. To make our defence we attack our prosecutor's credibility. So we tell often ourselves that the whole of the Old Testament is either out of date or too complex for us to understand. We harden our minds and suppress what is true.

But when we understand that Christ came to forgive us from law-breaking and to give us the power through his Spirit to start liking what is good for us, then we are able to "turn to the Lord", experience his blood-bought forgiveness and then recognise the clarity of the Old Testament for what it really is – God's loving truth for human freedom. In this way, by the Holy Spirit in Christian hearts, God begins to reverse the effect of the fall on human reasoning and enables us to see the world more clearly.

From this humbler position we are enabled to think about those parts of the Old Testament which commonly present ethical paradoxes. When we are reassured by knowing the generous God who died for us then we are willing to consider how to interpret such paradoxes with an open mind.

Christ resolves the complexity of the Old Testament

The interpretation of many aspects of the Old Testament is undoubtedly complex, such as the application of biblical law. But the Bible tells us the story of God's purposes in and for this world and Jesus is at the heart of those purposes. This means that the key to interpreting complexity is the unfolding of God's historical plan in relation to Jesus Christ. On that basis, David McIlroy noted six important points to bear in mind when interpreting the Old Testament.

1.   God hasn't changed.

This fundamental tenet of Christian theology needs no further explanation: "I, the LORD, do not change." (Mal. 3:6) "Jesus Christ is the same yesterday and today and forever." (Heb. 13:8)

2.   Human nature hasn't changed.

As Christ is constant, so is the natural order of creation, and humanity in God's image. This means we reject an evolutionist view of morality (i.e. what is good for us changes with our evolution) and a constructivist view (i.e. what is good for us is whatever we decide as a culture). Human spiritual and physical needs haven't changed. We need to be clear what we are *not* saying. We are not denying that we face new challenges in our increasingly technological culture, nor do we assume that the answers of previous generations of Christians were necessarily correct.

What we *are* saying is that it is not enough to argue 'We know better now.' We need to be able to show how our thinking is consistent with the teaching of the Bible and with what the Bible reveals to us about the constant nature of God and the constancy of human nature.

3. *The Hebrew Scriptures were given to a particular culture, to a particular people, at a particular time in history, living in particular circumstances.*

The Law of Moses, the Torah, sits within a context – the unfolding of God's messianic plan in history. So we need to understand the different parts of the Old Testament in the light of their original readers and genre – while recognising their universal authority.

As David McIlroy clarified:

> Whilst the Torah clearly contains provisions which were enforceable by judges, the Torah as a whole was not a legal textbook accessible only to priests and teachers of the law. Instead, the idea was that each community of Jews in a particular location, each household, would meditate upon the words of the Torah in order that they should live their lives in accordance with them without the need for judicial enforcement of them. The Torah was supposed to be a way of life for the Jews. ...

> The Torah is not a blueprint for society which has to be copied exactly. Instead it is a paradigm on which Christians should reflect, drawing inspiration for creative solutions to contemporary challenges. 'A paradigm is something used as a model or example for other cases where a basic principle remains unchanged, though details differ. ... A paradigm is not so much imitated as applied. It is assumed that cases will differ but, when necessary adjustments have been made, they will conform to the observable pattern of the paradigm.' [19]

4. *The Hebrew Scriptures were not just about foretelling but forth-telling.*

The writings of the prophets are not only prophecies showing that Christ would come. Part of their anticipation of Christ lay in their doing what he would do: they communicate God's unchanging character. So they contain universally relevant moral teaching. Chris Wright insists that "we need to study and classify the laws of the Old Testament against their own social background in ancient Israel and then discuss what significant moral features emerge within *every* kind of law they had." [20]

5. *Jesus is our guide to interpreting the Old Testament.*

Jesus taught that the two greatest commandments summarised the law: we should love God and we should love our neighbour. The law shows the outworking of love and this is how we should value it.

It is also by understanding Christ that we can "study and classify" Old Testament laws, and distinguish "significant moral features" from their other features, such as those whose typological function means they no longer apply in the same way today.

The law is a unified whole, and Christ as one man embodied all of it. But Christ's fulfilment of the law in different ways helps us understand how to use it in a variety of ways today. So, for example, the sacrificial system which concerned Israel's direct relationship with God now applies to us as the context for Christ's own death, once for all, and his on-going priestly work. Other aspects were designed to keep Israel distinct as a state from the surrounding nations with a consciousness of purity, for example the food laws and other civil separation laws. But when Christ came he expanded the church across all cultures – explicitly replacing the food laws with greater emphasis for us on a purity of heart and the ethical distinctiveness of the church. What remains is the summary to love God and neighbour and worked examples of what this looks like in a particular social context, in the light of the moral order of creation.

6. *Jesus did not come to found a new nation state but to establish a Church which would be present within all nations on earth.*

There are theological differences between the Old Testament state of Israel and modern states today. Theirs was a unique period where God's people were identified as a single nation state, as if church and state were combined. To study Israel as a model nation requires us to distinguish those features which were unique to its theocracy, rather than imitate them. We are used to making such distinctions: Christ acts as a model human for our example but he is also unique as the only Saviour and Judge; the only one to whom every knee will bow.

Objections to the Bible as public truth

Many objections to the Bible *per se* are made by its opponents, for example, that it is not authoritative, that it has an unreliable manuscript record, that it is just a record of human thoughts about God (rather than revelation from God through divinely inspired human authors), that the Old Testament still contains morally repulsive elements, that it cannot be reliably interpreted, and that any texts cannot reliably convey an author's meaning to a reader.

It is not within the scope of this study to rehearse a general defence of the Bible against post-Christian suspicion or to demonstrate why it consistently transforms individual lives, families and cultures across the world. Other resources adequately address these concerns to restore confidence in the Bible. Suffice it to say here that Christian confidence in the integrity of the Bible is as relevant to the public square as it is to the spreading gospel. Either the Bible is trustworthy or it is not, regardless of whether it is used for our private lives or our public lives. It would be inconsistent to hold to one and not the other: they stand or fall together. But some objections to the Bible specifically relate to its use as public truth:

"The Bible is not a political textbook."

Objectors argue that, instead, the Bible is a book about how to relate to God. But this objection falsely divides truth. God created all of life and speaks to all of life. Relationship with God and with the world is entwined. Any quick overview of the Bible shows that the whole book is about the whole of human experience dealing with creation and law, with kings and with peoples, with history, administration, agriculture and justice. Of course, it needs careful interpretative reading, and so it doesn't just give contemporary quick fix solutions – and in that sense it is of course unhelpful to refer to the Bible as a political textbook. But it is not a misuse of Scripture to ask of it social and political questions, and it answers them in the wider context of God's plan for the spread of the gospel, seen most clearly in God's revelation in Christ.

"We should use sociological studies not the Bible."

Ultimately these should not be in opposition to one another. Our aim is to understand the world the way God has made it – the way it really is – so that we can flourish in accordance with its own order. By saying that the Bible is the highest and clearest authority in this endeavour we do not discount all other efforts to understand the world as it is. Because the same reality is communicated by general revelation through nature, and special revelation through the Bible, we expect that the two will cohere with one another. Indeed, by reading the world, we read the Bible better, and vice versa. This requires patience and careful work. We should not take the reliability of sociological evidence for granted or use it uncritically – truth is unified and so bias can affect everything. But nor should politicians change the legal *status quo* to reflect new fashions which are not shown to be good for society by solid evidence.

"People won't listen if we quote the Bible."

An authority is not necessarily a language. It is not integral to the Christian position to quote the Bible in order to promote policy. On the contrary, because the Bible extends and clarifies what God has already revealed in creation, we are able to talk about the world we all share in terms that everyone can understand. When we speak in the language of God's general revelation – creation – we are no less speaking in God's language than when we speak in terms of special revelation from the Bible. That is not to say that reference to the Bible in public is unacceptable. But the concern of the public authority is action for the public good. The Bible may or may not be a tool in the front-line discussion of this action: its helpfulness will depend on the context.

"The wars of religion show the Bible is politically unusable."

Of course, historical arguments (on both sides) usually suffer from over-simplification and from cultural presuppositions. To what extent were the politics behind the "wars of religion" driven by the Bible itself or by the medieval tradition of Christendom and the usual clash of local competing political interests? And might not today's simplistic blame of the Bible *per se* actually reveal the atheistic worldview sitting behind those parts of the academy and the media which seek to silence the Bible's claims?

On the contrary, the central problem behind the 'religious' element of the wars of religion was the *lack* of biblical engagement. This is seen in the medieval failure to untangle church and state institutions. As a result, institutional division within the church was wrongly thought to necessitate political division between states. But this was a contextual problem not a biblical problem, and it would be anachronistic to raise it now. The Bible had been only recently rediscovered and distributed. Instead, the religious wars represent the demise of the unbiblical church-state system of medieval Europe which had developed in an age where the church institution rather than the Bible represented the supreme source of public truth.

"But not all societies have the Bible for public truth, and not everyone is a Christian."

This is a theological argument that God would not reasonably expect non-Christian societies to depend on the Bible for public truth. The objection's logic appeals to common grace: public authority does not depend upon the spread of the gospel for its existence and it is to be accessible to non-Christians. Therefore it would be inconsistent of God to give public authorities their task without access to all the relevant epistemological resources. Thus, the objector concludes, the Bible cannot be a necessary provision of public truth.

But, first, God *has* provided the Bible to the world. Virtually no society today is without the influence of the Bible, even if this is an indirect and limited influence. That is, societies whose political systems have historically been shaped by a biblical influence have in turn influenced – to some degree – a large number of other political systems in the world, even if those societies don't have the Bible in their own language. The Bible has irrevocably shaped the conscience and composition of today's world in ways the world itself does not readily acknowledge.

However, we admit that while the world does benefit from the Bible's unacknowledged influence, the Bible itself is a closed book to any people who are not at the same time engaging with Christ himself – not least because he is the interpretative tool for unlocking the complexity of biblical law, and because he reconciles us to its clarity.

So, we respond *secondly* by noting that the difference between a public authority's functional existence and its full maturity. By common grace, public authority can exist and perform basic tasks independently of the arrival of the gospel in that society. But it will never reach the position it ought to reach, just as humans themselves are limited in their private enjoyment of temporal life without the gospel. God has, in his wisdom, glorified the gospel by giving societies enough knowledge through natural revelation to keep themselves alive and generally make judgments to that end, and yet not enough knowledge to truly flourish without Christ and the benefits of the gospel.

As ever, we are reminded that we should not consider God's provision of public authority in complete isolation from his provision of the gospel and his plan for it to spread. The sphere of public authority was never intended to become an entirely self-sufficient sphere with the capacity to create a utopian society without need of the gospel.

The more the gospel spreads in a society today, the more its citizens will have access to the Bible. And if the Bible contains God's revelation concerning public benefit then, in one sense, all citizens can have law books in their living room – as we saw that Charles I discovered.

Conclusion

Revelation provides public truth. Society is indeed too complex and diverse for any single human conception of it, but it is not too complex for a unified divine conception. Human views of reality are indeed clouded by our subjective context, but the Creator's perfect view of his creation is definitive – we simply need to know what it is. When "God saw everything that he had made" and said it was very good, we ask: "what, in fact, did he see?" This question of public truth requires revelation from God, and Christ is his revelatory Word.

Christ's revelation in the Bible addresses both of the elements within the original question: first, "Is there such a thing as public truth?" and second, if so, "How can we know what it is?" Christ's role as the agent and template of God's act of *creation* makes it right to say that public truth exists and gives us a certain insight into its content. Then, because of Christ's *incarnation* and its record in the Bible we can know public truth clearly and in more detail because it has been revealed to us in writing.

David McIlroy left the following conclusion:

> We have been here before. Ours is not the first generation to be sceptical about the compatibility of human reason and divine revelation…

> If there is no connection between revelation and reason, then you end up with two serious problems. One is that it then becomes impossible for Christians to talk to anyone else about the implications of their faith. You can't explain why it is a good idea to stay married for life or to give away a tithe of your income. The other is that

God either has a split personality, so that creation has no connection with redemption, or, worse still, the implicit suggestion is that one sort of God made the world while another sort of God has acted to redeem the world.

What we need is an understanding of the limits of reason in the light of revelation. We are called to love God with all our heart, soul, *mind* and strength. God gave us our minds for a reason. He expects us to use them. We need to practice the disciplines of *obedient reason*, learning to use our reason to *think* about what it means to live an authentically human life, how to interpret the world around us, and how to interpret the Bible.

CHAPTER SUMMARY

2. Public Truth – How can we *know* what is 'good'?

The **government's mandate** requires public truth to promote the public good.

▷ We need to know about society in order to benefit society. Rule according to law stands on evidence and truth, not arbitrary whim, mere power, bribery, false witness or fashionable opinion. Truth promotes intellectual analysis, constructive discussion, diversity and the use of evidence.

▷ But humanity by itself only enjoys limited agreement on what it is true about human life. Even reliable social evidence can be difficult to identify, limited in specifics and variously interpreted. Different starting points can lead to different conclusions. Many are now cynical about 'truth' itself and are ready to abandon its necessary place in the rule of law.

The **gospel's message** tells of Christ who is the truth. He reveals truth by creation and incarnation.

▷ As Christ is the *logos*, all things were made through him and so reality is coherent, rational, knowable and communicable. His general revelation through creation is the ground of all knowledge and truth, whether people realise it or not. Common grace means that, to an extent, sinful humans still have a sense of what is good and evil for all of society – but because of the fall and our finitude we are limited and need further revelation.

▷ By Christ's incarnation, recorded in the Bible, we see Christ's special revelation of himself. The working out of the gospel reverses the effect of the fall on human thinking. By turning to Christ, we are enabled to use the Bible for what it is, and what history shows it to be: the only authoritative and reliable source of public truth. The Bible clarifies and extends what we see of the creation order, especially through a careful Christian reading of the Old Testament.

3. PUBLIC GOOD

So what *is* 'good' for us?

What is good for society? If people are designed by God to thrive, what should we know about God's design so that public authorities can encourage human flourishing and avoid working against the grain of God's workmanship? What is the *content* of the public good?

Creation is structured to flourish in life

Creation order from the beginning

"God saw everything that he had made, and behold, it was very good." This resounding statement completes a structured series of seven where God creates and evaluates: "And God saw that it was good." The seventh adds "*very* good" once human life had been created as the crown of God's work.

'Creation' is not just 'nature' in the sense of the 'natural world'. It includes humankind and their role as God's representatives to rule and be fruitful within it. This will include culture and human association. Everything in human culture in that respect reflects something of the goodness and the potential of God's created order.

Jonathan Chaplin re-established the doctrine of creation as central to the question of the public square:

> The key to the biblical doctrine of creation is not to do with biological origins – of course there is a lot to say about that but that seems to me not the thrust of what the Bible has to say about creation. Rather, the central thrust is to teach us

the comprehensive scope of God's will for the whole of human life, indeed the whole of reality, and to teach us about our radical dependency on his sustaining power and love and law. To confess 'I believe in God, the Creator of heaven and earth' is to confess that all human creatures inhabit a shared reality, designed and sustained by one God, pronounced 'very good' in Genesis chapter 1.

This shared reality is a *structured* reality. It is not a coincidence that 'good' is repeated seven times within a structured account of creation paying attention to the production of 'kinds' and the creation of the seven-day week. There is a proper ordering and purpose within this structure of kinds – waters are for the sea, the sun is for the day, birds are for the air, fish are for the sea, fruit is for food and humankind (male and female) is to multiply and rule over it all under God. It is this designed, structured reality which is very good.

Consequent to creation's structure is its *fruitfulness*. "Let the earth bring forth living creatures according to their kinds" is typical and reaches its climax in the structured mandate to humanity: "So God created man in his own image, in the image of God he created him; male and female he created them. And God blessed them. And God said to them, 'Be fruitful and multiply...'"

As the infinite life of the Trinity overflowed to give *life* to the creation, creation has its own relational order for fruitfulness and the multiplication of life in itself. So when we are identifying the public good, we are identifying God's design which provides for human flourishing and the burgeoning of *life* itself.

Creation order still has universal authority

God's structuring of creation was maintained after the fall. God upholds his original order of creation in the face of human sin and rebellion. God maintains that order, he maintains human nature, he maintains the image of God in all human beings in spite of our turning away from him. Consequently Noah was given the renewed mandate to "be fruitful and multiply" and the dignity of human life in the image of God was reasserted after the Flood.

While the Bible teaches that "creation itself groans" and exhibits disorder as a result of the curse, this merely reinforces the abiding importance of the creation order. The proliferation of weeds and the painfulness of childbirth only act as curses because men and women are still here to enjoy the earth's fruitfulness and to flourish together with children.

Therefore the life-multiplying creation order of Genesis remains the pattern for our good. As Jonathan Chaplin summarised:

> We need to recover a confidence in God's design of creation order as being the very best for human beings. We are tempted today to feel like an embattled minority in an encroaching secular world. ... We are fearful that our perspective on the world is just a tribal perspective, that it is an idiosyncratic perspective that has no possibility of being recognised or defended, or commended in the public realm. But if God's creation design is indeed what it claims to be, if it is universal, if it is the condition for a flourishing human existence, if it is the route towards *shalom* then it is not just that for Christians, it is that for all human creatures. So what we have to share with other people is not a gnostic insight – it's the truth about their own human nature...

But how does the rest of the Bible shed light on the goodness of creation and its life?

Creation life is the subject of redemption

God did not abolish creation at the fall because God's plan is to restore it by *redemption*. When Christ returns there will be a renewed creation: the new heavens and a new earth (2 Pet. 3:13, Rev. 21:1), where the Greek for 'new' implies 'renewed'. Then we will see the fulfilment of God's original design of humanity, ruling over creation in perfect fellowship with God. Psalm 8, which celebrates the structured creation narrative, turns out in the New Testament to be a prophecy of the world to come (Heb. 2:5-9). The creation of humanity and its exalted role in dominion over the whole creation thus becomes an anticipation of Jesus' exaltation as the second Adam. As the head of a new humanity Jesus has been given the kingly rule over all things, and his people, his own human brothers and sisters, will rule with him. No wonder the end of Revelation echoes the beginning of Genesis.

So the story of the *kingdom of God* is the story that God's good rule over creation, mediated through humans, is being permanently re-established. Ever since Adam was expelled from paradise, the earth has suffered the consequences of human enmity against God. God's good rule over creation is not mediated through humanity when humanity rejects it. Rather than life, the result has been death through the misrule, mismanagement and unnecessary suffering with which we are all so familiar.

So the kingdom of God is *good news* for the world, because where God's rule is restored, the earth rejoices. This will be seen in its fullness when the King returns in person, inaugurating the new creation.

Creation life was patterned in the promised land

The coming kingdom was to be pictured by the history of Israel. Specifically, the promised land was to serve as a miniature of the whole creation rejoicing in fruitful life under God's rule through his rescued people. While all the other nations of the earth groaned under the curses of fallen humanity, the land of Israel would be a beacon of redemption hope under God's good rule.

Creation life ordered by God's law

God's life-giving rule was to be mediated in the land through the *law*. God gave Israel his orderly laws, statutes, testimonies, commandments and precepts, and by applying them the people would experience the fruitful life for which they were created. As they stood on the other side of the Jordan, poised to enter the promised land, Moses recited the law and called the people to obedience. In God's law they had life, so obedience was urged upon them: "Now choose life, that you and your children may live." (Deut. 30:19 NIV).

When Moses finished reciting all these words to all Israel, he said to them, "Take to heart all the words I have solemnly declared to you this day, so that you may command your children to obey carefully all the words of this law. They are not just idle words for you – they are your life. By them you will live long in the land you are crossing the Jordan to possess." (Deut. 32:45-47 NIV).

God's laws are "not just idle words" for us either. In them the good ordering of life in God's creation is spelled out. For Israel, the law was a unique privilege because as God's revelation it acted as the means by which his rule could be restored over creation. No other nation had laws like it. For us, the law is a privilege too because we can now eavesdrop into that same divine ordering for a flourishing life in creation. In the words of Jonathan Chaplin:

> The Old Testament law is a uniquely authoritative revelation of how the people of Israel were to live within the design of creation. ... Torah pointed the people of Israel to a way of life, or ways of life, that are in conformity with God's original creational design. ... We should interpret the law as a specification of creational design for that particular people. ... Its authority is not bound by its context but transcends it... It is a unique insight into God's universal design for the whole of creation.

Biblical law is precious indeed. God's law was rightly prized by our believing forefathers both in ancient Israel and in the legal development of much of the West. Today we can rediscover its riches. In the law we are told about our neighbours so that we can love them, and about ourselves so that, all other things being equal, we can live a long and peaceful life. We are given insights into how social relationships and structures should ideally operate. Even by the law's variety of sanctions we can begin to identify those aspects of social structuring which God has designed to be more fundamental.

Creation life for every family

By way of example, we can explore the law of jubilee from Leviticus 25.

If Israel in the promised land acted as a miniature of restored humanity ruling over creation, then each Israelite family served as an even smaller microcosm of the whole, within its own plot of land. Just as the new creation will be given to God's rescued people, so the promised land was given to a nation of former slaves, and within this land God gave a specific and perpetual allocation of land to each household. Thus, free families were to live together on their own fruitful land which they could work, enjoy and pass down to their children.

The jubilee principle acted to maintain this pattern of creation life against the degenerative effects of sin over time in this cursed world. It did so every fifty years by a miniature repeat of God's restoration of freed slaves to their original land, thereby providing a repeated picture of all humanity's future hope.

In practice the jubilee worked through a principle of inalienable family land tenure combined with the more familiar principle of redemption. The plot of land given by God would be kept in the family in perpetuity. If a family fell into hard times they would become separated from the free enjoyment of their land, either by selling it or, additionally, by selling themselves to become the 'slaves' (more like bonded employees) of their creditors. If, after up to fifty years, either the land or the family had not already been redeemed by their relatives, then the sound of the trumpet heralded their restoration. The law ensured both the people and land were redeemed without money and with no strings attached. This took place in a Sabbath year of rest which reminded the people that they were set free from slave labour to enjoy God's world. So once again the freed slaves could enjoy God's creation life as he intended, no doubt praising God all the more for his gracious ways, past, present and future.

Insights for today

The jubilee offers a resource for much fruitful meditation. As a start, we might suggest that the permanently valid principle underlying it was that it was good for every household (extended family) to have ownership of sufficient productive resources to give the family economic independence. Integral to this vision was the family's work on that land, just as Adam was given the garden, and humanity is to care actively for creation. This allowed for generosity and it encouraged family stewardship of creation, because a man's land was not only for himself, but for his family and descendants. As a result this fostered a sense of rootedness, and the whole picture ensured that families lived in proximity to one another and were able to provide and care for one another's welfare. Such a developed picture of creation goodness irrepressibly reminded the people of God's goodness to them and inspired their free worship to him.

Jonathan Chaplin then suggested two high-level applications by way of example. First, the jubilee points against extensive state ownership or control of the productive resources on which people depend. This observation is coherent with what we saw in Romans 13 – the expectation is that the principal acting agents of society are the people themselves, rather than first of all the state. Secondly, the jubilee points to the protection of the economically vulnerable. How that protection works, and who provides that protection is a complex question: but it should be on our agenda because the Torah is marked by its consistent provisions to ensure protection for the poor.

Using biblical law in this way requires serious thinking. Mainstream Bible teaching has not been engaged in this kind of publicly-orientated thinking for many generations, and it may therefore seem unfamiliar and daunting to us. But rational reflection and serious intellectual work is fitting in the light of what we know about the nature of public truth from the last chapter. And in the Bible God reassures us that he doesn't expect us to find all the answers automatically. We are reminded in the Psalms that the godly are those who *meditate* on the law of the LORD both day and by night, and that when we do, we will prosper in life like a fruitful tree planted in God's good creation (Psalm 1). So God's laws are "more precious than gold, than much pure gold" (Psalm 19:10).

This 'day and night' meditation in Leviticus sounds challenging. But we should be encouraged to recognise that in these particular applications of the jubilee principle we have certainly moved beyond the basics. Indeed, we will always find that our biblical path leads us to deeper things which need further meditation before we can put them to use for the public good – and rightly so. But while some things are not immediately clear, others leave the reader in no doubt, and it is important to start with the basics.

Basics of the public good

The same can be said of the 'golden' jubilee principle. However we may choose to mine its depths, certain basic truths shine clearly on its surface. The public good is seen in free families living together in physical proximity, with resources which they can use for work, enjoy and pass down to their children. In this simple picture we see the foundational elements of the creation narrative introduced in Genesis which are later reaffirmed throughout Scripture.

Some key features

So we can provide a guide to some key features of the goodness of the creation order, traced from Genesis 1 and 2 and the jubilee vignette. Humans are designed to enjoy *life* in God's world sharing equal status together as God's representatives caring for creation. God has created them *male and female* to have *children* and to be fruitful together in the lasting and stable *family* life centred in the public structure of lifelong monogamous heterosexual *marriage*. The delight of faithful sexual union celebrates this bond and also brings fruitfulness. God has instituted such family life in the context of the extended family, as the basic unit of public life and welfare. Children's primary duty is to their parents, who correspondingly have primary responsibility for them. As God's ruling representatives, people should steward resources productively for the benefit of others, prioritising their own children and relatives. To do so they should have ownership of their own *property* without stealing from others, but trusting others and trusting in God's good provision. Humans are not defined by their work but should enjoy contented *rest* and experience the *freedom* to live in the world God has graciously given them. This should be a freedom without slavery or harm so they can volunteer to their Creator their heartfelt *worship*.

The Ten Commandments

Notice how this simple account effectively repeats the vision of the Ten Commandments which, in this context, emerge as God's own ten-point guide for a long and flourishing life in the creation he has given us to live in and care for. This explains why they act as a summary of the key principles of public love and serve as his starting point for the law in Exodus 20, and again as the starting point in Deuteronomy 6 when the law is repeated. They then reappear by allusion throughout the prophets. Little wonder that many Western political buildings were built – including the US Supreme Court – displaying the Ten Commandments as a symbol of life-protecting law.

It is helpful that God's ten-point guide is expressed in moral injunctions. They give us a handle on how to move toward the universal good through the specifics of our particular situation. In other words, the language of moral command has a practical epistemological advantage: how we know what to do. We may not always be able to see the whole divine conception of the public good and its relationship to where we stand in any given moment. How then do we pursue the public good? Moral commands work with our God-given sense of personal responsibility and accord with our conscience. When as officers of the state or private citizens we do what is right and help others to do the same, with reference to those commands, we can be confident *that* we are at the same time working for the benefit of ourselves and those around us. It may only be later that we fully understand *how* what was right was also good. At all times we remember from chapter 1 that in relation to society, our use of the moral order is for society's benefit, and that this does not equate to an anti-gospel sort of moralism.

The Ten Commandments act as a significant affirmation of human freedom, not least because – ironically – they are mostly presented in the negative. Adam was created with God-given freedom to enjoy Eden. The trees were there for him to eat any fruit he chose, except that he should *not* eat from the one tree which was forbidden. Similarly, God gave his people freedom to live, and the role of the law – "you shall not" – was to protect, not curtail, this corporate freedom. It is only when life is thought to be provided by law, rather than by God, that the negatives of the law seem to be a restriction of freedom. This is an important distinction to keep in mind so that our positive vision of human life protected by law is not communicated as a vision of negatives, which will be interpreted as moralism. The message of the Ten Commandments is that there is more to life than law and that's why law can protect it.

The enjoyment of the public good

So a final aspect remains. The Ten Commandments ensure we don't ignore the role of the *human heart* in the enjoyment of the good. Israel was given freedom to leave the political tyranny in Egypt in order to have the space to worship God, ultimately in the promised land. Their final enjoyment of the land was grounded in their enjoyment of the God who gave it to them. The Ten Commandments commence with a statement of this motivation and with the worship of God, and they conclude with the significance of trusting contentment. Thus, interwoven throughout the social provisions of the Torah is the constant theme that human freedom exists *for* the enjoyment of life in a trusting and free relationship with God.

The Feast of Ingathering was a spectacular call to divine enjoyment. It was to be held at the end of the fruit harvest as a celebration of thanksgiving. Families were to enjoy feasting and the novelty of living outdoors in little shelters constructed from fruitful and fragrant green branches (which was why it was also known as the Feast of Tabernacles, or Booths). The children especially would have enjoyed making the booths:

On the first day you are to take branches from luxuriant trees – from palms, willows and other leafy trees – and rejoice before the LORD your God for seven days. Celebrate this as a festival to the LORD for seven days each year. (Lev. 23:40-41 NIV)

They were to rest and do none of their customary work. It was a multi-sensory reminder that once they were once slaves and then homeless travellers on their route out of Egypt – but now God had lovingly placed them in a fruitful land with the freedom to rest and to enjoy living with their Creator. He had given them a peaceful and quiet life for all godliness and holiness. This is the opposite of a killjoy. God loves to see the people rejoicing and so they are warmly reassured:

Be joyful at your festival – you, your sons and daughters, your male and female servants, and the Levites, the foreigners, the fatherless and the widows who live in your towns. ... For the LORD your God will bless you in all your harvest and in all the work of your hands, and your joy will be complete. (Deut. 16:14,15 NIV)

Human enjoyment of God is socially relevant. We notice here that the abundance of divine enjoyment overflowed to include the immigrants, the poor and those who had no family. God's generosity had given his people good land, and this would inspire generosity to others around them. Their experience of God became a key motivation to use their freedom to treat the poor kindly, to protect the vulnerable and stand up for those who were oppressed as they had been. Such encouragements within the Torah generally do not operate within the sphere of legislative requirement, but simply set out the expected fruit of a thankful *heart*.

So the *human heart* provides the final piece to the jubilee jigsaw itself. In the context of an approaching jubilee, where a plot of land would revert to its original owner, people could take economic advantage of one another by failing to buy or sell at a fair price as measured against the length of time before the next jubilee. But the appeal not to do so relied chiefly on the expectation that a divinely rescued people would be God-fearing. Similarly the reason they could afford to rest in the jubilee year was because they trusted contentedly in God's provision for them, and they didn't need to work without a break.

The people's heartfelt enjoyment of God provided for their enjoyment of the good land he had given them. Their joy and thankfulness was to overflow in heartfelt generously to the vulnerable so that in the context of family based personal relationships *everyone* could enjoy the land. Their fear of God protected against artificial pricing, and their trust of God gave them a healthy work-life balance because it provided the base of contentment.

So the role of contentment demonstrates that the trusting human heart can sustain the public good in lean seasons, in that deprivation does not inevitably result in stealing and social disorder – as the prophet Habbakuk experienced:

> Though the fig tree does not bud
>   and there are no grapes on the vines,
> though the olive crop fails
>   and the fields produce no food,
> though there are no sheep in the pen
>   and no cattle in the stalls,
>   yet I will rejoice in the LORD,
> I will be joyful in God my Saviour.
> (Hab .3:17-18 NIV)

Conclusion

Life to be protected

The Bible's picture of ordered human flourishing offers an attractive and coherent vision for our neighbours. It has stood the test of time throughout human history because in his love our Creator God has carefully designed and structured human life to flourish.

What does this mean for law today? Putting together all our conclusions so far, we can say that the core mandate of public authority
is to protect and maintain the public structures of life that God has
provided. What is our starting point for this action? As ever, we take
our lead from God: we begin law where he begins it. The presumption must be to start with God's own ten-point list for his people's
good – as our forefathers have done. So we can repeat and re-group
these ten principles and the following serves as an illustration of
how this might be done to provide the most basic framework of law
and wider public policy in promotion of the public good:

Protection of freedom (first to fourth commandments)

▷ Humans should be free under the law to enjoy worshipping
their Creator in the way that he commands, and they should
be free to speak about him in a way that reflects his honour
(Deut. 6:7-11). How is this freedom to be protected by law?
The concern of public authority is public order. So historically
the freedom of religion has provided an umbrella of freedoms
which accord with it, and under which both worshippers and
non-worshippers can shelter, such as the freedom of speech,
freedom of association and freedom of conscience. The freedom of religion, properly understood, is the keystone for all
human freedoms. (By 'properly understood' we mean that this
is not a self-defining absolute but sits within the wider biblical framework and is therefore subject to a prohibition on
child sacrifices and any other 'religiously demanded' crimes.)

▷ Humans should have freedom from slavery to enjoy these
God-given freedoms (Deut. 6:6, 12-15). Therefore freedom from slavery should reach beyond merely the abolition
of modern-day slavery found across the world – though it
should not be less than that, and there is much to be done on
that front. But humans should not be compelled to over-work
but have the freedom to enjoy rest at least one day in seven.

Protection of family (fifth and seventh commandments)

▷ Marriage is a fundamental public unit, a publicly declared life-long exclusive covenant between one man and one woman glued together with sexual union (Deut. 6:18). Marital sex is thus precious and fruitful. Extra-marital sex ultimately harms people because it acts against the human physical, emotional and social design, it undermines marriage and it undermines society. Marriage should be promoted and protected by law.

▷ Children should have a father and a mother so they can be blessed in honouring them and parents should have primary responsibility for their children (Deut. 6:16). This provides basic principles for good policies and laws in relation to bioethics, adoption, education and welfare.

Protection of human life (sixth commandment)

▷ Human life is the most basic goal of the public good, yet it is fragile and should be protected by law from murder and harm (Deut. 6:17). Government should therefore protect life against violence internally (e.g. by police) and externally (e.g. by armed forces), and prohibit acts such as abortion and euthanasia. In all these areas we recall that the love of the magistrate is first for society corporately, within which, rather than contrary to which, he loves individuals.

Protection of property (eighth and tenth commandments)

▷ Ownership of property should be enjoyed contentedly and owners should be protected from theft (Deut. 6:19, 21). This speaks to the protection against robbery in all its forms, and governs the handling of economic regulation. It also reminds us that it is good for every family to have access to productive resources and a part to play in fruitfulness.

Protection of justice (ninth commandment)

▷ Truth should govern the work of justice (Deut. 6:19). Witnesses should be required for any conviction. This speaks to the arrangement of the courts and biblical law shows that people should be considered innocent until proven to be guilty.

These basics are increasingly necessary today. Each simple principle recounted above stands against the flood of contemporary Western culture which seeks to redefine God's structures and calls 'good' 'evil' and 'evil' 'good'. The corridors of power are populated by many who say there is no Creator. As Romans 1:22 delineates, "claiming to be wise, they became fools." In biblical terms, a fool has false confidence in his own wisdom, and when pressures come – such as economic strain or social unrest – he finds himself to be weaker than he thinks. The same can be true of a culture. Today we are moving away from God's good *life* and instead, in our confusion, we are shredding our own fruit before it can flourish, and even pursuing what we now call 'good death'.

So we can love our neighbours in two ways. We can help society arrange itself in accordance with the universal biblical order for flourishing human life, which we have seen throughout this chapter.

Life – more abundantly

But we can also use this vision, as the jubilee was used, to point people to the good news of the Lord from whom it all came and who gives us enjoyment of it all. This is the Creator who entered the cursed creation for its restoration, and who announced the jubilee to his own neighbours when he arrived:

> The Spirit of the Lord is upon me,
> because he has anointed me
> to proclaim good news to the poor.
> He has sent me to proclaim freedom for the prisoners
> and recovery of sight for the blind
> to set the oppressed free,
> to proclaim the year of the Lord's favour.
> (Luke 4:18-19 NIV)

By his message, all humans everywhere can now participate in an even greater and more joyful experience of divine rescue from slavery than Old Testament Israel.

Jesus taught that all of us are slaves to sin because although we can have freedom to make our own choices, we find our hearts habitually choose many things which harm us (John 8:31-36). But the truth of Christ's jubilee message sets the human heart free on the inside. This enables us to enjoy our political freedom on the outside, which in turn overflows with generous and contented social implications – and ultimately to pursue freedom for those who don't have it.

Jesus said, "I have come that they may have life and that they may have it more abundantly." (John 10:10 NKJV). We can feast on the abundance of his household (Ps. 36:8). This life keeps us going through hard times, and makes us fruitful in many other ways even if the life of blessing pictured by Old Testament Israel is not open to us in this life, for whatever reason – and it finds its complete fulfilment in us only at his return. Jesus is *life*, and we can share in it for eternity because he *died* for us. He is the *good* shepherd who lays down his life for the sheep – the Creator bearing creation's curse as he hung on one of its trees.

We can't miss the relationship between the goodness of creation life and the good news we spread. As Jonathan Chaplin concluded:

> Christians need to recover a biblical doctrine of creation from neglect. ... It is a neglected theme but it is the foundation of the gospel, it is the foundation of the Bible. Unless you understand Genesis 1 and 2, the rest of the Bible is diminished in its significance. The point of the gospel is diminished in its significance as well.

CHAPTER SUMMARY

3. Public Good – So what *is* 'good' for us?

The **government's mandate** involves the legal protection and promotion of the good structuring of flourishing life.

▷ In the Mosaic law the public good is patterned by free extended families living together on their own fruitful land which they can work, enjoy and pass down to their children. This picture acts as a God-given paradigm from which important underlying principles can be drawn for policy today.

▷ Key protections for the public good can be summarised in the legal protection of human freedoms, family, life, property, and an honest process of justice.

▷ Although public authority should protect and promote the fruitful structures of life, in itself cannot provide true enjoyment of this life.

The **gospel's message** tells of Christ who is the life – the source, pattern and goal of abundant life.

▷ God, through Christ, is the origin of all life, the provider and definition of all good. He is the creator and the re-creator of human life forever.

▷ Christ's rescue from sin paves the way for abundant life which begins in the heart. This inner life then overflows to bear fruit in family and social life, and ultimately aspires to provide the same social freedoms for humans everywhere.

▷ The inner life brought by the great jubilee of the gospel brings joy and contentment which give social stability in times of austerity, and social generosity in times of abundance.

4. PUBLIC HOPE

How can this 'good' be *achieved*?

We have seen what is good for human flourishing, but how is that good to be achieved? How much should we expect of the public authority? How should we be involved as Christians?

The hope of creation is – and has always been – for the re-intervention of God's saving rule mediated through humanity. This was lost by Adam and his descendants' sin: we rebel against God's rule. But the good news of the kingdom of God is that God's own Son has – by a very public love – intervened and become the second Adam whom God has now exalted as creation's King. Through him all humanity can be reconciled to God's rule as each individual comes to believe in him. Believers then mediate the benefit of Christ's rule by the Holy Spirit through our hearts guided by his word to promote the good of the world around us. Through him, we ourselves can intervene in love to help a dying world. Although God's saving rule grows now as every new believer turns to Christ and is filled with the Holy Spirit, the full restoration of all things can only take place when creation's King returns and intervenes personally for a second time, at the sound of his final jubilee trumpet.

Peter preached this same good news publicly before being arrested by the rulers:

> Repent therefore, and turn back, that your sins may be blotted out, that times of refreshing may come from the presence of the Lord, and that he may send the Christ appointed for you, Jesus, whom heaven must receive until the time for re-

storing all the things about which God spoke by the mouth of his holy prophets long ago. (Acts 3:19-21).

So our hope in Christ's rule is twofold. When Christ returns he will restore all things to God's good order for new creation life which will be eternal. In the meantime he is able to send times of refreshing to this creation through his Spirit's presence in repentant believers as he rules in our hearts.

Christ's rule as the King of love has implications for rulers and for Christians in general.

Implication for rulers: justice

Humility

Political rulers have a tendency to great pride, forgetting they are merely God's servants for our good. They may claim to pursue the public good by blowing their own little trumpets – or, in the case of Nebuchadnezzar, by playing his horn, pipe, lyre, trigon, harp bagpipe and every sound of music, upon which all peoples, nations and languages were expected to worship his golden image.

The folly of such pride is recounted from Genesis to Revelation, from the confusion of Babel to the fall of Babylon the Great. Right in their midst God exposed such kings – who are pictured almost comically through the prophet Daniel as being little horns with mouths which speak boastfully of great things. These are they who bring their own rule to the world, rather than co-operate with the restoration of God's rule. So they are pictured as having the wisdom and sophistication of 'beasts' not of men, and Nebuchadnezzar himself was humbled by God to eat grass like an ox. Animals cannot compete with the Son of Man, and in the face of their reign, creation's hope is entrusted to the second Adam:

> I saw in the night visions,
>   and behold, with the clouds of heaven
>   there came one like a son of man
>   and he came to the Ancient of Days

and was presented before him.
And to him was given dominion and glory and a kingdom,
    that all peoples, nations, and languages should serve him;
    his dominion is an everlasting dominion
    which shall not pass away
    and his kingdom one that shall not be destroyed.
(Daniel 7:13-14)

Therefore the self-styled 'divine' world empires – Babylon, Persia, Greece and Rome – all fell, and the statue which represented them in Nebuchadnezzar's vision was knocked down by a stone which grew into a mountain and covered the earth. This stone was not cut by a human hand, but it was chosen by God and precious. And so Christ becomes the chief cornerstone and his kingdom, re-establishing God's rule, will stand forever.

Thus the role of today's public authority is decidedly *secondary* in the story of the world. The main story is not about human authorities but it is the story of the gospel spreading across the world in anticipation of the new creation. It is the gospel that changes people's hearts and minds and thereby society and those in authority – because *God's* rule is the salvation of the world. And so the final good will not be achieved without the appearing of the King himself. Earthly kings, presidents and governments must humble themselves. They are not the answer to all the world's problems. They are not the depositories of all good things. They are not the Messiah. As they take the stage they should tone down their rhetoric and their walk-on music.

Wisdom

How should public authorities take a lower stage and learn how to rule from the greater plan of God's kingdom? Where does this fear of the LORD take a ruler? It provides wisdom to do justice.

King Solomon advised: "The fear of the LORD is the beginning of wisdom, and the knowledge of the Holy One is insight." (Proverbs 9:10). But this is unpopular:

> Why do the nations rage
>   and the peoples plot in vain?
> The kings of the earth set themselves,
>   and the rulers take counsel together,
>   against the LORD and against his Anointed, saying,
> "Let us burst their bonds apart
>   and cast away their cords from us." (Psalm 2:1-3)

Pride sees God's laws as chains to autonomy not insights for blessing, and so the boastful little horn will instead "speak words against the Most High, and shall wear out the saints of the Most High, and shall think to change the times and the law..." (Dan. 7:25). In recent times, for example, the post-Christian West has experienced political law-changing which seeks to alter God's fundamental ordering of creation. Even human life itself is becoming redefined, leading us, like Nebuchadnezzar, to become animal-human hybrids. Wisdom does not try to redefine or bypass marriage and family life in an effort to achieve good ends by another means.

Instead, God's wisdom sets the agenda for wise rule today. Wisdom's skill brings the imperfect ordering of this world back *towards* conformity to God's creation order, rather than lend order's strength to establish alternatives which are contrary to God's paths of life. Unwise rule may know that love provides order, but may forget that such order must be *good*. Wisdom's task is to recognise the relevant features of creation's order and bring the situation toward it skilfully.

Justice

In other words, wise rule brings freedom through *righteousness and justice*, which is the constant call of the Old Testament. These are a pair because righteousness (Heb. *tsedeq*) is conformity to God's life-ordering, and justice (Heb. *mishpat*) is the intervention required to achieve it. Or, more precisely, justice is "the action that needs to be taken in a particular situation to place people and circumstances in conformity with *tsedeq*". [21] So justice is only justice when it is grounded in the righteousness of God's own ordering for life. But when the wise judge brings true justice he can be confident that he is contributing to *freedom*, because freedom is found where we were created to flourish. The springs of creation life become blocked when artificial structures are established as alternatives to God's own natural channels. But when we use God's law, justice can flow like rivers, and righteousness like an ever-flowing stream.

Since justice is active, it is not sufficient for rulers to have laws. Rulers need to *intervene* with justice to improve and implement them. The implementation of law is not easy and this is why it flows from humility: injustice often occurs in the places where rulers find it easier not to go. But Christ is the model of a king taking the form of a servant, and humbling himself even to the point of death – in order to intervene and achieve justice for the poorest of all.

Realism

Justice also recognises the *limitation* of public authority – lest in its pursuit of justice it should trample human freedom. This limitation is felt in two ways.

First, justice cannot make choices for other people. Although public authority can arrange life's channels, we have seen that it cannot bring life to people's hearts. It can punish evil and encourage good but it cannot create good or extinguish evil.

Within public protection, people have the freedom to live their own lives and worship God (or choose not to do so) and to bring blessing to society through their own lives and families (or choose not to do so). Sadly people often choose not to do so because human sin has diseased our hearts with folly, and we use our freedom to make harmful choices.

How can the authority respond? For a government to *make* people choose wisely for themselves is to choose for them and so gradually remove their freedom. Public authority needs to rely on something else, within people's hearts, to cause them freely to make good choices for themselves. But without that humble reliance, the pride of the public authority starts to encroach into every area of life, family, education, business, association and worship, and the presumption is that everything is a matter for public authority and little is left to people's freedom.

Second, society's harmful choices may leave the public authority with *tied hands* and limit its provision of justice. Where an authority rules with the consent (or even direction) of the people, the people may refuse to accept God's ordering for their good – which they see as chains to their autonomy. The authority is then very limited in bringing 'justice' because there is another standard for what is regarded as 'righteousness'. Where this is the case the authority starts to lose legitimacy as it can no longer punish evil and encourage good. If instead it then rules without the consent of the people then it tends to lose its effective legitimacy anyway. Such a society is so far from the gospel that it is also effectively also moving towards lawlessness. It urgently needs the good news to open its eyes to good laws.

Prayer

In recognising such limitation, the ruler who trusts God has a hope which points him *beyond his own sphere*. Like Daniel, he takes a private interest in the growth of God's greater kingdom and the welfare of God's people, recognising that creation's hope is found in the rule of the Son of Man. While seeking the welfare of the city in which he lives, he is also known to pray earnestly and regularly for the City of God which is his true home: "your kingdom come, your will be done on earth…"

For anyone in public authority today, such private prayers will inevitably contribute to a sensitivity in policy making, helping them to see how to shape public policy in a way which encourages those who do good. This will mean taking an active private interest in understanding how public life can be ordered such that Christians and Christian charities can more easily flourish in good works, and being sensitive to the evils which threaten them. This is not to give Christians any favourable treatment or to combine church and state. On the contrary, the issue is methodological. By understanding which policies allow God-ruled people to do good and to live peaceful and godly lives, the ruler has an insight into the public good for all of creation. This is what will be best for everyone else too, and should be argued as such.

Encouragement

As the ruler prays that God's kingdom will come, he finds God's kingdom gives encouragement.

Justice is *manageable*, not hopeless. Government is not required to provide life to society, but only to order it so that the life of God can flourish easily within it. Males and females don't need the government to give them children – God himself has given life to humanity. But this life is protected when murderers are punished and marriage is encouraged. The same is true of God's redeeming life through the gospel. People don't have public authority to give them spiritual life – they are born again through the living word of God which is preached and exemplified by his church and its radical life of discipleship. Heart change is not the job of the public authority. But this new life is certainly protected when the rule of law gives people the freedom to preach, witness and worship.

Justice now is only *temporary*. Although judges are to bring God's wrath to the evildoer, and not just the wrath of society (Rom. 13:4), Christ is the man God has appointed to bring final and perfect judgment. He is the *logos* of creation and will come again, in judgment, to declare truly what was good and evil within his own creation order, and will reorder with it eternal consequence. Before then, temporary judgment represents a very serious, but not a crushing, responsibility. We must use our wisdom as well as we can in complex circumstances to bring justice for the public good, but we can trust Christ ultimately to judge human all hearts and put all wrongs to right.

Justice is *understandable*. God teaches the humble his ways including kings who recognise God's greater kingdom. From this they can derive understanding about earthly kingdoms, benefitting from the public truth of the Bible. Only through God's kingdom can we fully account for the proper role of public authority within wider human life – providing a coherent framework for authority, truth, goodness and hope – because in Christ are hidden all the treasures of wisdom and knowledge.

Challenge

Christ is King. He is not only the one human who has been promoted to heaven's throne, but he is also divine as God's beloved Son. He is the greater reality to which the ancient kings arrogantly aspired. And he will return to do justice. Although this gospel is good news to the humble, it is also a frank declaration of a rival and superior rule to those who stand against it. The gospel says that the pride of human rulers – who trumpet themselves before Christ's final trumpet – is at once laughable and deadly serious. Psalm 2 continues:

> He who sits in the heavens laughs;
> the LORD holds them in derision.
> Then he will speak to them in his wrath,
> and terrify them in his fury, saying,
> "As for me, I have set my King
> on Zion, my holy hill."
> I will tell of the decree:
> The LORD said to me,
> "You are my Son;
> today I have begotten you.
> Ask of me, and I will make the nations your heritage,
> and the ends of the earth your possession.
> You shall break them with a rod of iron
> and dash them in pieces like a potter's vessel."
> Now therefore, O kings, be wise;
> be warned, O rulers of the earth.
> Serve the LORD with fear,
> and rejoice with trembling.
> Kiss the Son, lest he be angry, and you perish in the way,
> for his wrath is quickly kindled.
> Blessed are all who take refuge in him.
> (Psalm 2:4-12)

Rulers are urged to submit to Christ's superior rule, and, as it were, kiss his feet in an act of homage. This repentance and recognition of Christ's Lordship is at once salvation for their souls and the beginning of political wisdom. Their requisite action is then to do justice: to humbly, wisely, actively, prayerfully, and realistically intervene according to law on behalf of those suffering harm.

Implication for Christians: love

A newly converted and zealous politician may hope to bring the benefits of God's rule directly to the nation merely by introducing the right set of laws. The same hope may be tempting for other Christians.

King Jesus rules through hearts

But it is vital to remember that God's rule is no longer mediated directly through constitutions or documents of law which can be written on stone or printed on paper. Israel's history showed the limitations of perfect laws: the people didn't keep them. God revealed his new constitution, the new covenant, to Daniel's contemporaries:

> I will put my law in their minds and write it on their hearts.
> … I will give you a new heart and put a new spirit in you;
> I will remove from you your heart of stone and give you a
> heart of flesh. And I will put my Spirit in you and move you
> to follow my decrees and be careful to keep my laws. (Jer.
> 31:33, Ezek. 36:26-27 NIV)

God's rule is now brought through the writing of his law on human hearts. People in the dark enter the light of his kingdom by being born again of the Spirit.

This means the nation state is not the vehicle of Christ's kingly rule. Instead he rules through the hearts of his people wherever they live. So at Pentecost where the church was established, Christ sent his Spirit into the hearts of people gathered from every political region and language as they repented and believed in him. His rule is now international and supra-national.

The arrival of the Spirit was the proof that Christ had been enthroned as King in heaven, and that he would return as such. He has not yet returned but is already reigning through believers' hearts as they flourish with the fruit of his Spirit. We are now in the age when God's future kingdom is breaking into the present. The Holy Spirit is the first experience of eternal life in the renewed creation: he is the guarantee of our promised inheritance.

Far from being withdrawn, God's saving rule has become personal. Believers look to Christ by faith and Christ joins himself directly to their hearts by his Spirit. As a result of this permanent connection, Christian activity is really the work of the King: it is the fruit of the Spirit, which is Christ-like *love*. Love is the fulfilling of God's law, whose summary is to love God and to love our neighbour as ourselves. Put another way, the Old Testament law shows us what neighbour-love looks like in God's creation, and now the Holy Spirit gives Christians the inner desire and the power to fulfil this good vision of joyful life in God's world.

Thus Spirit-filled hearts are God's direct agents for social transformation. The hope of the modern nation state is the flourishing of Christianity within it. And this means that lasting change requires the printing of Bibles more than constitutions, the work of missionaries and not just mandarins, and more pastors than presidents. The hearts and minds of the people need regime change as they become Christians and then channel Christ's rule of love to their neighbours.

Love for our neighbours

But who should experience these overflowing blessings of Christ's rule? Perhaps this should be limited to members of the church community as we await Christ's return from within our Christian bunkers?

No. Christian love should overflow to society in the same way that Israel was called to be a light shining to the nations, with its wise laws inspiring wonder from its neighbours. Foreign royalty was drawn to Jerusalem by the wisdom of God's king and the riches of his ways – it took their breath away. So from God's throne righteousness and justice were to spill beyond the boundaries of God's people to fill the whole earth with the joyful demonstration of his glory. This is now the calling for Christian love as it flows from the fountain of life through our own hearts in streams of living water, accompanying the spread of the gospel which has been commissioned for all the nations.

So if we are asking 'who is my neighbour?' the parable of the good Samaritan gives the most expansive definition of 'neighbour' possible: we ourselves are neighbours to whoever needs our love. If Christ's Spirit is within us we should expect to love as Christ did. This means laying down our lives for our remotest enemies not merely for our closest friends. It also means that, regardless of their stance toward Christianity, we pray for kings and all in authority, and we are called to show them practical love.

Wayne Grudem summarised this memorably:

> If someone were to say, 'Wayne, why are you going around speaking on Christians' involvement in politics and government?' – if I only have one sentence because it is just a brief conversation, and I have to answer quickly – I will say:

> 'Because Jesus commands us to love our neighbour as ourselves.' And if I love my neighbour I want good laws for my neighbour: laws that will protect my neighbour's marriage, laws that will protect my neighbour's children, and their upbringing and their moral training, laws that will protect my neighbour in other ways and do good for people's lives, not laws that will oppress and harm people.

> So the command to 'love your neighbour as yourself' implies that we should work for good laws and good government.

The principal hope for the public good is the multiplication of Christian love and its impact on society and the public square. We are saved by grace, through faith, to do good works and these good works are to shine like a light to the world bringing glory to God and honouring the gospel of the King.

Significant Christian influence

True love aspires to bring "significant Christian influence" in the public square. It means influencing the public square to return to its God-given mandate. There are many positive illustrations of how Christian love has influenced governments across the world throughout history. From Pentecost to Rome, the book of Acts charts the growth of the early church which would make its presence felt in the Empire as a whole. In the words of Wayne Grudem:

> ...Christian influence on government was primarily responsible for outlawing infanticide, child abandonment, and abortion in the Roman Empire (in AD 374); outlawing the brutal battles-to-the-death in which thousands of gladiators had died (in 404); outlawing the cruel punishment of branding the faces of criminals (in 315); instituting prison reforms such as the segregating of male and female prisoners (by 361). [22]

The same pattern has continued throughout world history wherever we see the spread of genuine Christianity – the rule of Christ by the Holy Spirit through the faith of sincere believers. We might think of well-known examples such as the abolition of slavery in the British Empire through the work of the devout Christian William Wilberforce, who was also a leading founder of the Church Missionary Society. There are also less well known examples, such as the prohibition of burning widows alive in India (1829). This campaign was led by William Carey, the missionary who founded the Baptist Missionary Society. Similarly, as the China Inland Mission brought Christianity to China, Christian influence led to the outlaw of the painful and crippling practice of binding young women's feet (1912).

As we love God and love our neighbours across the world, we want to see the rejoicing of the nations bringing glory to God. So we pray for our endeavours:

> May God be gracious to us and bless us
> and make his face to shine upon us,
> that your way may be known on earth,
> your saving power among all nations.
> Let the peoples praise you, O God;
> let all the peoples praise you!
> Let the nations be glad and sing for joy,
> for you judge the peoples with equity
> and guide the nations upon earth.
>
> Let the peoples praise you, O God;
> let all the peoples praise you!
> The earth has yielded its increase;
> God, our God, shall bless us.
> God shall bless us;
> let all the ends of the earth fear him! (Psalm 67)

Common objections

"But won't political involvement distract us from evangelism?"

This takes us to the heart of the relationship between public authority and the gospel – which has been the scope of this whole study. Sovereign love shows that we love our neighbour by *both* evangelism and practical action. We should challenge the presupposition behind this objection and consider the diversity of gifts and callings within Christ's church. As Wayne Grudem clarified:

> The proper question is not, 'Does political influence take resources away from evangelism?' but, 'Is political influence something God has called us to do?' If God has called some of us to some political influence, then those resources would not be blessed if we divert-

ed them to evangelism – or to the choir, or to teaching Sunday School to children, or to any other use. ... The whole ministry of the church will include both emphases. And the teaching ministry from the pulpit should do nothing less than proclaim, 'the whole counsel of God' (Acts 20:27). It should teach, over the course of time, on all areas of life and all areas of Bible knowledge. That certainly must include, to some extent, what the Bible says about the purposes of civil government and how that teaching should apply to our situations today.

This means that in a healthy church we will find that some people emphasise influencing the government and politics, others emphasise influencing the business world, others emphasise influencing the educational system, others entertainment and the media, others marriage and the family, and so forth. When that happens, it seems to me that we should encourage, not discourage each other.

"Isn't it doomed to failure? Isn't everything getting worse?"

Wayne Grudem noted that our attention is often drawn to the signs of the end of the age in Matthew 24, but continued:

> I believe that there will be a time of greater persecution yet to come before Jesus returns, *but I don't know when* that's going to happen. I don't know if it will happen next year or ten years from now or a hundred years from now or three hundred years from now. What I do know is that in the meantime I'm to be obedient to the teachings of Scripture, and what I do know is that there is a possibility that as we work, and as we are faithful, and as we trust God, instead of persecution we may see revival.

Dr Grudem pointed out that between 1950 and 2010 the number of born again Christians has increased from being 3% to 12% of the world's population. Dr Grudem shared that, personally, he suspected that God would not abandon the West but that revival would yet come. He said that Christian lawyers, for example, can prepare for revival by working, amongst other things, "to influence the legal system and the government to give space for the gospel to be preached." Other ways to prepare directly for revival would include work to protect the freedom of churches and Christian organisations to hire Christians. More generally, Christians should want to see all areas of law reflect what is good.

"But wouldn't some old fashioned persecution be good for us?"

Jesus' response was: "No". Jesus teaches us to pray: "Lead us not into temptation, but deliver us from evil." Paul, in 1 Timothy 2 encourages us to pray for good government, so that God preserves our freedoms such that the gospel and obedience to the gospel might still continue in our lives. We shouldn't pray for illness, and shouldn't seek persecution. God's sovereignty may indeed turn bad situations to good, but this should make us love the good all the more. Christians with the experience of real persecution would find the suggestion perplexing from the lips of other believers. Persecution is not only bad news for the church but also for our neighbours – and we care for them.

So how do we go about it? How do we lovingly bring Christ's blessings to assist and reform government, and move toward significant Christian influence?

Seven principles of public love

We have now come full circle – we are seeking to walk in the paths of Sovereign Love himself. When we clear our way to bring love to the public square we uncover Christ's own footsteps before us and we join him in his work from the beginning. We often forget that Christ was a very public figure. His public love is our pattern for what we do and how we do it. His example presents a constellation of seven principles to guide our path, enabling Christians in different circumstances to develop their own particular strategy within the same biblical framework.

1. Grace: love brings goodness not moralism

God's *grace* provides both the gospel and public authority. Public authority is to love society by commending what is good and punishing what is evil. This was the message of chapter 1: love and morality are not mutually exclusive.

So our contribution to public policy is to follow God's lead in the role of public authority. Christ did not come throwing stones, and he would not even break a bruised reed. Likewise we should graciously set out what is good for human flourishing based on the creation pattern. This is "very good" news to bring to our fellow men and women. So we lovingly participate in public authority by applying public truth to promote the public good with public hope. In so doing we multiply pictures of grace.

It is a tragedy when Christian political involvement misrepresents God by moralism. Our policy contribution is *not* to be the condemnation of sin but the provision of benefit. Certainly, love in the public square must involve recognition and correction of sinful policy, but our specific policy concern is not primarily sin but harm. As love corrects harmful policy it shows sincere concern for society, taking no delight in identifying wrong, but rejoicing much more in what is good.

But shouldn't Christians in public life lovingly point out society's *sin* – not just its harm – so that people will accept the gospel?

2. Carefulness: love makes careful distinctions for each situation

We love people truly when we see them for who God has made them to be, and carefully interact with them accordingly. Jesus' interaction with people illustrates love in this way: his responses are different to different people in different situations. God has made a *distinction* between public authority and the spreading gospel – the government's mandate and the gospel's message. So when addressing public authority as public authority, we do so lovingly by recognising its God-given role and speaking to it in its God-given terms, helping it do what God has given it to do. This means we are drawn to make a careful distinction between *policy* and its *context*.

The *context* of policy is the story of the kingdom of God, and this is the gospel. For example, the authority of government is delegated and defined by God's sovereign love; the truth we apply to develop policy is ultimately founded on revelation; the criminality we punish is caused by sin; the good we commend is derived from God's creation; the hope for social transformation is genuine Christianity. These gospel features make sense of the public square but they are questions of the public context and not of public policy.

But *policy* itself is more limited – it is the job the government is called to *do*: it is the daily business of the public authority. So one of the benefits of God's distinction between policy and context is that, due to common grace, to a certain extent people who give vastly different accounts of the public context (e.g. whether life is sacred in God's image) may nonetheless *act* together on policy (e.g. that murder is a crime). To this extent common grace makes a firewall between political philosophy and policy so that when human sin causes the fragmentation of philosophy this does not automatically result in the disintegration of the public authority that God has lovingly instituted for humankind.

So love learns with *wisdom* when a given situation requires the wider gospel message, and when it is more helpful to bring a policy contribution alone. The gospel has not replaced the on-going role of the public authority. As Wayne Grudem vividly pointed out:

> Is it true that evangelism is the *only* means that society should use to stop drunk drivers? 'I know you've been driving drunk; let me share the gospel of Jesus Christ with you and see if your heart will change.' Well, no, I would recommend rather that the policemen arrest the drunk driver, put him in jail and when he has sobered up then you can share the gospel with him... But God uses *both* the gospel and the power of civil government to restrain evil: *two* means.

We should beware of *reductionism* which turns these 'two means' into one. In political discussion reductionism confuses public policy and its gospel context. In constitutional structuring, it can lead to the merging of church and state institutions. But the church institution is to teach the message of the kingdom of God, while the public authority is to implement public policy for our good.

This distinction should shape the *corporate Christian contribution* to the public square. When Christians together want to preach the gospel to public authority they should do so as the church, and follow Paul's example to preach the whole counsel of God. John the Baptist himself did not shrink from calling King Herod to repentance. However, when Christians feel called to devise and promote the details of policy they should not do so in the name of their churches but should set up charities or societies to do so as Christian citizens. God's wisdom here provides for greater efficiency in policy contribution and will also help to ensure that people who don't believe in Jesus do not confuse their local church's gospel with a certain political policy. Churches should not become the arms of political parties. It is also true that Christian para-church organisations or societies should not be confused with churches.

God's distinctions enable different Christians to pursue the different *callings* God has given them. We might suggest that God called Billy Graham to evangelism and William Wilberforce to give his life, amongst other things, to the abolition of slavery. Similarly, some Christians will be called to bring Christian love to the public square from within the government and others from the outside. We should encourage other Christians in their own callings especially when they are different from our own.

So whenever love speaks in the public square it takes account of the particular situation: who is being addressed, and by whom, and then considers what will be most helpful in the circumstances – whether to work mainly with God's common grace or whether to proclaim his gospel grace too. But either way, the Christian contribution is *gracious*. So if, when discussing public policy, love demands a frank discussion of the social context in the light of the gospel, we must do so boldly and faithfully, but never delighting to declare the nation's sin, but rather pointing it to its Saviour. We extol the riches of his grace as we mourn over our corporate and individual sinfulness.

3. Service: love comes not to be served

Jesus said "The Son of Man came not to be served but to serve." (Matt. 20:28). The authentic Christian contribution to the public square is not self-serving as if we are a besieged special interest group. Christ the Servant King is reigning – and reigning through us. So we are here, unafraid, to seek the peace of the city and over-flow the blessing of Christ's rule to our neighbours.

God's ordering of *creation* makes this love possible. As we saw in previous chapters, what we have to share with society is not a tribal perspective but it comprises the universal conditions for human flourishing revealed by God. By bringing public truth to bear on public policy for the *public good* we are not promoting a 'Christian' vision narrowly defined, but a universal vision from the Creator for the benefit of his creation.

In practice this is complex. If Christ's rule is the hope for our nation, then love for the nation must seek to protect the Christian contribution to society. But if society is to understand this it must first experience the impact of Christian love. Thus when Christianity is in decline it can feel that the battle for public policy is a vicious circle: Christianity is needed because… it is needed.

But here we return to what is *good* for society. If Christianity consists in the healing of broken humanity to an increasingly restored humanity then Christian freedom is really human freedom. If a law has the effect of curtailing Christian freedom then it denies true freedom to everyone else too – perhaps without them realising it. We should therefore interpret every threat to Christian freedom as a threat to freedom *per se*, and, in policy terms, defend it on that basis. Particular circumstances require careful thought as to how service can be authentic both in substance and presentation. But the starting point of Christian policy is not to argue for Christian privilege but human protection.

Public policy must not be confused with private help. Paul tells the churches: "as we have opportunity, let us do good to everyone, especially to those who are of the household of faith." Part of the church's blessing to society is its model of love to one another. We are fellow citizens bound by the ties of heaven. So the *church* should give especial assistance to its members passing through the same justice system whose improvement *Christian policy makers* promote for everyone's benefit.

4. Persuasion: love appeals with persuasion and evidence

However, society may not immediately recognise that good policy brought by Christians is indeed beneficial. Here the gospel trains us in loving *persuasion*. The nature of faith is something which cannot be compelled. Christ didn't seek to compel people into his kingdom but reasoned with them, publicly inviting people to seek their own benefit:

> Come to me, all who labour and are heavy laden, and I will give you rest. Take my yoke upon you, and learn from me, for I am gentle and lowly in heart, and you will find rest for your souls. For my yoke is easy and my burden is light. (Matt. 11:28-30)

Paul reasoned and persuaded in the marketplace, knowing that truth is public. Wisdom itself calls out by the gates of the city, urging the foolish to learn wisdom for their own good.

So in the public square we are called in the same way to persuade and reason with people about what will benefit them most. By creation we all share the same reality and so God has given us a common language of experience. The authentic Christian contribution within the public square is the reasoned discussion of beneficial policy, using the evidence of creation to demonstrate the truth of the Bible. God's world corresponds to his word – what he says works – so we can be confident that sound sociological study will support our loving arguments.

5. Patience: love endures opposition and misunderstanding

Surely everyone will warm to our grace, carefulness, service and persuasion? They will welcome the light we share? Sadly, not always. As Jesus demonstrated, even perfect love will be rejected. Opposition is not love's failure. Jesus couldn't be faulted, yet he was crucified anyway. John's gospel succinctly records the bizarre scandal: "He was in the world, and the world was made through him, yet the world did not know him. He came to his own, and his own people did not receive him." Jesus came with the life and the light of God, but the darkness of the world rejected him. "This is the judgment: the light has come into the world, and people loved the darkness rather than the light because their works were evil." (John 1:10-11; 3:19)

As servants we are not greater than our master: those who reject him will reject us. So even when we ourselves come with grace and truth to appeal persuasively about what benefits out neighbour, their reaction may well be driven primarily by their lost spiritual condition. We have already seen that as fallen humans we all have a disease of irrationality – sin – which causes us to love what harms us and to hate what is good for us, so we don't like the illumination of God's truth on these areas of our lives.

This means that if, for example, we are campaigning for marriage and family life as the best protection against poverty and the best basis for education then, even if we are speaking flawlessly in gracious terms of the public good rather than moralism, we should nonetheless expect to be unfairly accused of being bigots and moralists.

Jesus received opposition and insult with patience. We are called to do the same and to entrust ourselves to God who alone has an accurate assessment of our love. We should also understand what we are doing and why, so that we can give an answer to people who ask us for a reason for our involvement in the public square, and so that we can do so "with gentleness and respect, keeping a clear conscience, so that those who speak maliciously against your good behaviour in Christ may be ashamed of their slander. For it is better, if it is God's will, to suffer for doing good than for doing evil." (1 Pet. 3:15-17 NIV). So, opposition has practical implications:

First, we must ensure we really are doing good not evil. This is particularly important as a witness to rulers whose job is to discern, identify and commend those who do good – and we want their vindication not their judgment (1 Peter 2:14-17). We must be scrupulous to avoid giving any grounds to critics that we are merely moralists and instead demonstrate in every way possible that we are acting in genuine love for society. This may impact our strategy concerning which matters we prioritise and when, although our concern for how we might be perceived must never dictate the substance of love – we must still do what is good.

Second, we should not be too quick to accept or join in with accusations of moralism made against fellow Christians operating within the public square, lest we unwittingly join with God's enemies in their slander of his children.

Third, we are called to be realistic and to persevere. Wilberforce battled resourcefully all his life against slavery and for his success he remains an inspiration today. But we also remember that he did so in a nation which still operated within a Christian consensus, and the gospel has receded in Britain today. We need the courage and humility to be incremental – to employ wisdom to bring justice: to take the situation gradually nearer what is good, rather than thinking we can reach the good immediately. As Wayne Grudem noted:

> If persecution comes, then we trust God and we seek to be faithful to him no matter what the cost. But we hope and pray that it does not come.

6. *Evangelism: love cares for eternity*

Spiritual opposition shows society's need for the gospel. There is a danger that Christians can end up only "doing politics not evangelism." But God has given both public authority and the gospel. The danger for Christians in the public square is that we become ashamed of the simple gospel message itself. We might try so hard to be persuasive and sophisticated in our policy proposals that we start to feel the gospel itself is an embarrassment. Yet throughout his ministry Jesus consistently used his physical healings to point to eternal healing. Sometimes he even moved on from begging crowds to prioritise the preaching of his kingdom, and then he gave people hard sayings which divided the crowd and turned many away. Many thought he was mad, but others saw he had the words of eternal life.

Jesus shows that love cannot easily work for temporal benefit and keep silent about eternal benefit. Certainly love is careful to distinguish policy and its context. Our particular office or calling may not be one of full-time evangelism. We must be sensitive to the right time and place. But whether informally or otherwise we are always interacting with other humans whose eternal destiny dwarfs the significance of public policy. There will be a final judgment even of judges.

And so Christ's love compels Christians to bring the gospel to our fellow men and women individually as consistently and persuasively as we bring loving policy within the public square. As Christians we are not only channels for the King to rule through our hearts in actions of love for our neighbours. We are also Christ's ambassadors, as though God were making his appeal through us. "We implore you on Christ's behalf: Be reconciled to God. God made him who had no sin to be sin for us, so that in him we might become the righteousness of God." (2 Cor. 5:20-21)

7. *Action: love is zealous and brave*

Christ showed us that love takes action and intervenes for others to the glory of God. Moneychangers had recently moved into the only court of the temple reserved for the Gentiles, thereby turning their designated worship-space into a 'den of robbers'. Jesus was consumed with zeal for his Father's house. Not only did he risk his reputation by single-handedly confronting the moneychangers in the temple but this also led him to the cross, where his loving zeal consumed him completely and he faced the wrath of God on his own.

Action follows carefulness which makes it bravery. Jesus did not cleanse the temple on the spur of the moment but he did his reconnaissance the night before when he went into the temple and simply "looked around" (Mark 11:11). Likewise the cross was not an accident, but for thirty years he grew up and then for three years he spoke of his approaching death and steadfastly set his face toward Jerusalem. But when his time had come, his zeal blazed and its light now shines eternally for us.

Some of us are predisposed to action without thought, and others to much thought without ever doing anything. We all need to help one another reach the maturity of our Christ who showed that brave love is both careful and zealous.

This study has demonstrated the need for careful thought. We have sought to clarify common misunderstandings that actively working for justice, law reform and the centrality of family life necessarily implies that we are thoughtless, cultural imperialists, judgmental moralists, theocratic fanatics or somehow weak in relation to the importance of the gospel message.

If we have cleared a pathway for love we are now called to walk in it. Ultimately, the only thing to hold us back is our lack of love for the people around us. Let's pray that, by his Spirit, our King will share with us his zeal to love our neighbours and our enemies. And then, entrusting ourselves to him, let's take action.

Conclusion

Perhaps this final point is an indictment to many of us for our failure to get involved in public life. Whether or not we realise it, a failure to engage in public life is nothing more than a lack of love for our neighbours – who will end up suffering as a result. If Christians don't speak, it will leave a vacuum and the results will be extremely harmful.

The priest and the Levite walked by on the other side. When religious hypocrites fail to love our neighbour we find ourselves convicted by Christ's strongest words of criticism while he was on earth. Woe to us, hypocrites, if we do not get involved, if we do not use our gifts and education to take proactive steps to protect our neighbours by engaging lovingly with the public square including with our Members of Parliament and our local authority.

Christ as the hope of the world

We are called to be channels of Christ's loving rule and to love our neighbour as ourselves. As Wayne Grudem concluded, he noted that all believers have an obligation to be informed, and to vote and therefore seek to influence government in a good and positive way.

> But it might be that some of you tonight, as I speak, find in your hearts that God is calling you to devote more of your life, perhaps to seek to serve in political office, perhaps to seek to serve in some governmental agency or some other area of service, or perhaps to help Christian organisations in some campaign. If God is calling you to do that, I encourage you to do that because the need is great.

What we have to bring is good news. The sovereign love of God is good news. It brings good news to human life now and eternally. It means that getting involved in the public square in an authentically Christian way will, under God, not only bless our neighbours' temporal lives but also improve the conditions for the reception and spread of the gospel. Let's bring the whole good news of Christ.

4. Public Hope – How can this 'good' be *achieved*?

The **government's mandate** requires humble intervention through the action of justice.

▷ Public authority is not divine: it should not herald salvation but do justice.

▷ The humble art of justice is to intervene and re-order unjust situations back toward increasing conformity with the good structuring of flourishing human life. This includes both the shaping of just law, and the application of it.

The **gospel's message** tells of Christ who is the way. His intervention in history re-establishes God's rule over creation through humanity.

▷ This means the primary hope of nations is the spread of true Christianity rather than political activity. Christ has come once, and he is coming again: this changes everything.

▷ This means Christians have the privilege and responsibility not only to imitate their King, but, by the Spirit, actually bring his love to intervene in a needy world, including by working in the public square for the sake of our neighbours.

▷ Christians are called to love their neighbours in the public square by significant Christian influence: by assisting the government to fulfil its God-given mandate and also by telling their neighbours the gospel of Christ's greater government for eternity.

CONCLUSION

Framework for the public square

Sketching out the framework

The wisdom of God's love and sovereignty are revealed in action together in Christ. Christ is the good news.

Through Christ as Creator, God's common grace brings blessing to our temporal lives as a limited picture of the fullness of his eternal life, which is brought to us through his special grace in Christ.

Human rule is a limited picture of divine rule. Earthly kingdoms rightly sit within, and are affected by, the more comprehensive story of the kingdom of God. They share the same *shape* so that the smaller points to the greater, just as humanity rules in the image of God. As man's creation in God's image paved the way for the incarnation, so the shape of the public square enables Christ's kingdom to grow within human kingdoms. And so we anticipate the day we will hear the final trumpet blast: "The kingdom of the world has become the kingdom of our Lord and of his Christ, and he shall reign forever and ever." (Rev. 11:15)

God's glory provides all four sides to the public square. In Christ he provides creation with authority, truth, goodness and hope. All four come through Christ's love for public life within earthly kingdoms, and they are realised more fully through Christ's love in the kingdom of God for eternity. Thus the public square hangs within, and forms a part of, the framework of the gospel plan of which it is an imperfect miniature. For those who find diagrams helpful we might illustrate this as follows:

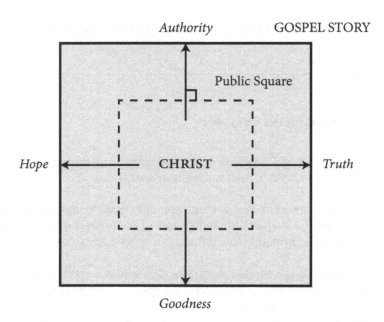

The diagram shows Christian love for society in action. Christ is at the centre as the source of everything. He is not only the spring of Christian love through the Spirit in our hearts, but he is also the one who gives it direction, because Christians know Christ to be the revelation of God's authority, truth, good life, and hope. This love is worked out through Christians to its ultimate goal in history. On its way it brings organic transformation. As it spreads it causes the public square (which sits within God's wider story of his own kingdom) to be increasingly aligned, in its own limited way, with the shape of God's own rule. This takes place as society's views about authority, truth, goodness and hope are brought more into line with reality.

These four aspects of Christ's glory provide the basis for practical policy in the public square in terms that everyone can understand. Being *public*, these four themes resonate throughout the history of human philosophy and they enable us to interact meaningfully with non-Christian insights.

Applying the framework

No earthly kingdom pictures the framework as it should. In reality, of course, we don't find straight lines and consistency. Every day experience may not feel like a public square at all. But as we walk in Jesus' paths of public love our task is to bring its distortion back into increasing conformity with the pattern of God's greater plan. This is the skilful task of justice – the task of wisdom. We do this by studying the kingdom of God and moving toward it through the coherence of evangelism and loving public action. In this way the good news of Christ brings the kingdom of God and corrects the public square in its slipstream.

In practice, this means that any given public question can be seen from its four perspectives of authority, truth, goodness and hope. It is likely that one or two of these themes will be the source of confusion for the particular issue in question.

When we've identified the issue, we can then trace how Christ is the source of that particular theme in creation and how it finds its fulfilment in the plan of the kingdom of God. And then we trace the issue back into the temporal realm of the public square. Theologically this allows us to situate policy between creation and the fulfilment of God's kingdom in the new creation. Practically it allows us to develop policy which will be coherent and accessible in the real world around us.

Discussing the framework

When as God's children we trace together the paths of Sovereign Love in this way we get to know our Christ more and more, and see his wisdom in creation and redemption. We love and admire him more, which is why we exist.

When we discuss political questions with people who don't believe in Jesus we can trace the same paths in our minds to provide consistent political answers. We can appeal to these four public concepts in language people can understand when the loving priority is to ensure the action of policy takes place. But as Christ's love compels us, and with the wise use of circumstances, we can take such a conversation organically to its logical implication – God's rule over the world through Christ. We might enquire of them how we deal with public authority's limitation. Or how do we really know what is true about society? What does it mean for something to be really good for the country? What hope do we really have as a society? In this way we love our neighbour by showing them Christ – using the sides of the public square as bridges to God's kingdom. We show people that in the public square we live and move and have our being in Christ.

The uniqueness of Christ

Christ is the framework for the public square. He coherently provides for our temporal and eternal needs. Christ is the basis and goal both of the public square and of the kingdom of God. He is Creator and our King. He is the Father's Word to bring us authority, truth, goodness and hope forever. When all is said and done, this study has done no more than paddle about in some of the implications of Jesus' own words:

"I AM the way and the truth and the life" (John 14:6)

Jesus uses the covenant name of the LORD – I AM – declaring his *authority*, and affirms that he himself is *truth, goodness (life)*, and *hope (the way)*. He surrounds the public square on all four sides. He stands under it and over it, in its midst and as its goal. So in anticipation of his glorious kingdom Jesus might simply have said: I am the public square.

What he did say is: "I am the Alpha and the Omega, the first and the last, the beginning and the end." (Rev. 22:13). Our right response is to fall on our faces before his throne and worship him as our Lord and our God, and then to say: Come, Lord Jesus! The whole story of humanity is encapsulated within Christ our God and brother. The riches of our King's wisdom take our own breath away. As Paul exclaims (Rom. 11:33-36):

Oh the depths of the riches and wisdom and knowledge of God! How unsearchable are his judgments and how inscrutable his ways!

For who has known the mind of the Lord?
    or who has become his counsellor?
Or who has first given to him
    that he might be repaid?

For from him and through him and to him are all things.
To him be glory forever.

Amen.

Further Reading

Good News for the Public Square seeks to provide a platform for further thinking in different areas and in more detail. It also seeks to provide a simple grid through which to benefit from other, sometimes contrasting, contributions to these topics in different contexts.

The following resources act as a representative introduction to a range of recent contributions, some of which include helpful bibliographies themselves.

Burnside, Jonathan, *God, Justice, and Society: Aspects of Law and Legality in the Bible* (OUP, 2011).

Chester, Tim, *Good News to the Poor: Sharing the Gospel Through Social Involvement* (IVP, 2004).

Chaplin, Jonathan, *Talking God: the Legitimacy of Religious Public Reasoning* (Theos, 2008).

Clark, Stephen (ed.), *Tales of Two Cities: Christianity and Politics* (IVP, 2005).

Green, Chris (ed.), *A Higher Throne: Evangelicals and Public Theology* (IVP, 2008).

Grudem, Wayne, *Politics According to the Bible* (Zondervan, 2010).

Gundry, Stanley (ed.), *Five Views on Law and Gospel* (Zondervan, 1996).

Haugen, Gary, *Good News about Injustice: A Witness of Courage in a Hurting World* (InterVarsity Press, 1999).

Keller, Timothy, *Generous Justice* (Hodder & Stoughton, 2010) and *The Reason for God* (Hodder & Stoughton, 2010).

McIlroy, David, *A Biblical View of Law and Justice* (Paternoster Press, 2004).

Sandlin, P. Andrew, *Christian Culture: An Introduction* (Center for Cultural Leadership, 2013).

Schaeffer, Francis, *How Should We Then Live? The Rise and Decline of Western Thought and Culture* (Crossway, 2005) and *Trilogy: The God Who is There, Escape from Reason, He is There and He is Not Silent* (Crossway, 1990).

Schluter, Michael, and Ashcroft, John (eds.), *Jubilee Manifesto: A Framework, Agenda & Strategy for Christian Social Reform* (IVP, 2005).

Schutt, Michael P, *Law and the Biblical Tradition: Select Bibliography for Christian Law Students (available online from the Christian Legal Society at www.clsnet.org)* (2001).

Spencer, Nick, and Chaplin, Jonathan (eds.), *God and Government* (SPCK Publishing, 2009).

Spencer, Nick, *Freedom and Order: History, Politics and the English Bible* (Hodder & Stoughton, 2012).

O'Donovan, Oliver, *Resurrection and Moral Order: An Outline for Evangelical Ethics* (IVP, 1986), and *The Desire of the Nations: Rediscovering the Roots of Political Theology* (CUP, 1996).

O'Donovan, Oliver, and O'Donovan, Joan (eds.), *From Irenaeus to Grotius: A Sourcebook in Christian Political Thought* (2000).

Wright, Christopher, *Old Testament Ethics for the People of God* (IVP, 2004), and *The Mission of God* (IVP, 2006).

Notes

1 Steve Jeffery, Mike Ovey and Andrew Sach, *Pierced for our Transgressions* (IVP, 2007).

2 David McIlroy, *A Biblical View of Law and Justice* (Paternoster, 2004).

3 David McIlroy, *A Trinitarian Theology of Law: In Conversation with Jürgen Moltmann, Oliver O'Donovan and Thomas Aquinas* (Paternoster, 2009).

4 Jonathan Chaplin, *Herman Dooyeweerd – Christian Philosopher of State and Civil Society* (University of Notre Dame Press, 2011).

5 Wayne Grudem, *Systematic Theology: An Introduction to Biblical Doctrine* (IVP and Zondervan, 1994).

6 Wayne Grudem, *Politics According to the Bible* (Zondervan, 2010).

7 Recent political developments are extremely complex, and in some senses perhaps more encouraging.

8 Quoted in Oliver O'Donovan and Joan Lockwood O'Donovan, *From Irenaeus to Grotius – A Sourcebook in Christian Political Thought* (Eerdmans, 1999), p. 142 (original translation from Henry Bettenson, Harmondsworth: Penguin Books, 1972).

9 "*The Homilies*" edition of John Griffiths revised by Ian Robinson (Preservation Press, 2006), p. 50.

10 Coluccio Salutati, *De Tyranno.1.*

11 *Policraticus* Book VII ch 17, edited and translated by Cary J. Nederman (Cambridge University Press, 1990) p. 190.

12 Thomas Aquinas, *Aquinas Selected Political Writings*, Edited with an introduction by A.P. D'Entrèves. Translated by J. G. Dawson. (Basil Blackwell, 1987), p. 81.

13 *Policraticus*, Book VIII, chs 18-19, edited and translated by Cary J. Nederman (Cambridge University Press, 1990), p. 205-207.

14 David McIlroy, "*Does the Law Need a Moral Basis?*" in Religion and Law, (Theos, 2012), p. 153.

15 Yoder, *The Christian Witness to the State*, (Herald Press US, 2002), p. 33.

16 Thomas Aquinas, *Summa Theologiae*, I-II.98.5.

17 John Calvin, *Institutes of Christian Religion* (1559) 4.20.16.

18 Geoffrey Robertson QC, *The Tyrannicide Brief* (Vintage, 2006).

19 Christopher Wright, *Living as the People of God* (IVP, 1984), p. 43.

20 Christopher Wright, *Old Testament Ethics for the People of God* (IVP, 2010), p. 288.

21 Wright, *Old Testament Ethics for the People of God* (IVP, 2010), p. 257.

22 Wayne Grudem, *Politics According to the Bible* (Zondervan, 2010), p. 49.